Waspleg
And Other Mnemonics

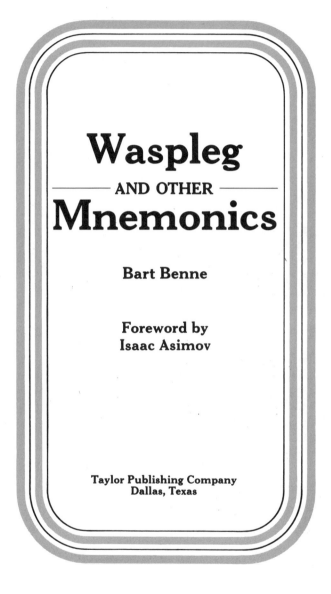

Waspleg
—— AND OTHER ——
Mnemonics

Bart Benne

Foreword by
Isaac Asimov

Taylor Publishing Company
Dallas, Texas

Illustrations by Paula Lawson

Grateful acknowledgment is made to Little, Brown and Company for permission to reprint lines from "The Tale of Custard the Dragon" from *Verses From 1929 On* by Ogden Nash. Copyright 1931, 1933, 1935, 1936, 1937, 1938, 1939, 1940, 1945 by Ogden Nash.

Published by Taylor Publishing Company
                1550 West Mockingbird Lane
                Dallas, Texas 75235

Library of Congress Cataloging-in-Publication Data

Benne, Bart L.
    WASPLEG and other mnemonics.

    Bibliography: p.
    Includes index.
    1. Mnemonics.   2. Study, Method of.   I. Title.
BF385.B46   1988   153.1′4   88-10766
ISBN 0-87833-616-8

Printed in the United States of America

10 9 8 7 6 5 4 3 2 1

To the Greek Goddess of memory
and
the mother of the nine Muses,

MNEMOSYNE

Foreword

We all have trouble remembering. It's a human curse. I am reputed to have an excellent memory, and I *do,* but even an excellent memory is full of holes. For that reason one has to employ tricks.

I was once courting a young woman whose phone number was 332-7378. Naturally, I had occasion to phone her frequently and it was annoying to have to look at a slip of paper to make sure I had the number right. But then I discovered, as I studied, the dial, that if I abandoned the number and dialed D-E-A-R-E-S-T, I got her. The word was easy to remember, and so appropriate, too, that I think I married her out of sheer relief at never getting the number wrong. And I still remember it today years after the divorce.

Of course, it could have its inconvenience. I was once dialing the young lady and something went wrong with the machinery and the operator said, "May I have the number you dialed, sir?" But I no longer remember the number I dialed. I only knew DEAREST. I said, "Wait a minute" and had to read the number slowly and painfully off the dial.

DEAREST is an example of a "mnemonic." You remember something that is difficult to remember by remembering something else that is easy to remember.

Of course, what is mnemonic to one person isn't to another. For instance, if I were told that someone's street number was 1603, I would have no trouble remembering it at all. I would say to myself, "That's the year Queen Elizabeth I died." But how do I remember that's the year that Good Queen Bess died? Well, I just do. It happens to be in my long-term memory and I might as well make use of it.

When I see the mnemonics that *other* people use, I sometimes wonder if it wouldn't be easier to remember the thing itself. I keep having this fantasy of someone saying that he's having trouble with the order of the ten most populous cities in the world. Someone else will say, "You mean you can't remember them." He will then answer, "Of course, I remember them" and he'll rattle them off perfectly, "but I've forgotten the mnemonic!"

And, indeed, nothing is perfect. The telephone dial has no letters associated with the numbers 1 and 0, so that it's often impossible to convert phone numbers into appropriate words.

Things change, too. When I was a kid, it was easy to remember the ten departments of the Cabinet and the order in which they might succeed to the presidency. One simply remembered "St. Wapniacl" and that gave you State, Treasury, War, Attorney General, Postmaster General, Navy, Interior, Agriculture, Commerce, and Labor. But what happened? Army and Navy were combined into Defense; new departments were added; and the order of succession to the presidency was changed by Constitutional amendment. It isn't worth remembering St. Wapniacl anymore, but I can't forget it.

But let's get to the book you're holding. Bart Benne has listed every mnemonic there ever was in every field. A lot of them he has made up himself.

There's no point in trying to read this book as though it were a novel. You might have no use for many of the mnemonics. Do you care about the order of the twelve cranial nerves, or the order of the spectral classes? Probably not.

However, as you leaf through the book, you will find some that you might indeed find useful. Or if you come across something that you need to remember, you might check the book in the appropriate chapter and see if a mnemonic already exists. Again, by studying the mnemonics (some of which may amuse you) you will get the notion of how to make one up for yourself. (And if you do, send it to the author. He may put out an enlarged second edition some day.)

But most of all tell yourself this. This is an absolutely unique reference book. There is nothing else like it in the world and if you find something useful here, then in all likelihood, you would be unable to find it anywhere else.

Doesn't that make you glad you own this book?

Isaac Asimov

Table of Contents

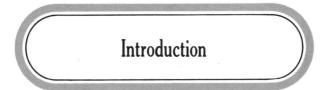

Introduction

This book might have been titled *How Do You Remember?* In almost every case when I have asked someone if they use any mnemonic devices or memory aids for remembering things they answer, "No, none that I can think of." But as we explore the subject further, virtually everyone discovers something, usually buried at a subconscious level, that they use.

This indicates two things. Almost everyone uses mnemonic devices of some kind. When you ask a child to repeat the alphabet you will most often hear them break into song with "lmnop" pronounced as if it were one word and some form of "Now I've said my "A, B, C's—tell me what you think of me." added at the end. Secondly, every person that I have discussed this subject with at any length has become enthusiastic about it and wanted to contribute in some way. People enjoy using memory aids and would like to learn more of them. Research has shown that students who use mnemonics learn faster, remember more, and get better grades than students who do not use them. The fact that you are reading this introduction confirms that you are interested in the subject.

Many of the words or phrases illustrated in this book are well known and in common usage. About one-third are original, others have been modified to make them more logical or presentable, some come from previously unpublished sources. All of them are designed to help you remember facts or concepts that may be important or entertaining to you.

I have used a very general interpretation of mnemonic devices in this book. I have included words, sentences where you use the first letter of each word, sentences and poems where you count the number of letters in each word in order to remember a number, images, anagrams, acronyms, and rhymes within the various sections which are organized by category. You will find examples of every method I know of to help you remember things.

By the way, the word "mnemonic" is not familiar to most people. Some of the synomyms that I have encountered are learning aid, memoria technica, memory aid, memory jogger, memory trick, mental checklist, mind game, quick study method, and study shorthand.

One reason for the popularity of mnemonic devices is that they force the material to be learned into an already existing framework of existing knowledge. You must know the alphabet before you can remember that a group of names are in alphabetic order. I did not realize how extensively mnemonic devices are used in the education of the learning disabled until recently. See the chapter on English Usage for a discussion of some of the methods employed.

Where I know who created a mnemonic device I've given specific credit in the text. When I know who first told me about a device or when they have gone out of their way to pass one on to me, I've given credit in the acknowledgements.

Obviously, the best mnemonic device is one that works for you. Your wife may have been in the Clio literary society in high school, so that may be an easier way for you to remember the muse of history. Brad Sham, the Dallas Cowboys radio announcer, remembers telephone numbers by associating them with Cowboy jersey numbers. He has the numbers memorized because of his broadcasting responsibilities. If it works, use it. What you will find here are devices that are as generic as possible.

This book does not attempt to teach you how to be a memory expert. It provides many examples of ways of remembering things. If it entertains or instructs you at the same time—so much the better. I would be very interested in hearing from any readers that use mnemonic devices that are not listed here. Please see the acknowledgements for the address to send them to.

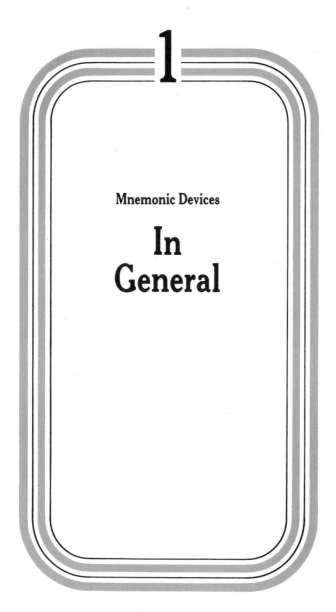

1

Mnemonic Devices

In
General

Every field of endeavor has certain facts or concepts that merit committing to memory. The examples included in this section defy any easy categorization. They represent a good cross-section of the different types of devices you will find in subsequent chapters.

The seven deadly sins may be remembered by using each letter of the word—

WASPLEG

W — Wrath
A — Avarice
S — Sloth
P — Pride
L — Lust
E — Envy
G — Gluttony

I choose this as the title of the book because it is catchy and I am known as a minor expert in each of those areas. I had originally intended for the illustration of this device to be on the cover of this book, but I was told many people will not buy

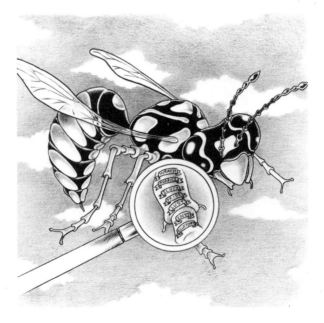

a book with a large, hairy insect on the cover, so it wasn't a good idea from the sales aspect. I had to insist, though. I think she's cute.

In order to give the forces of good equal time you can remember the four cardinal virtues with—

Try Putting Justice First.

T — Temperance
P — Prudence
J — Justice
F — Fortitude

The CIA uses an acronym to list the most common reasons why spies defect, but it works both ways—east to west and west to east—

MICE

M — Money
I — Ideology
C — Compromise
E — Ego

The OSS—Office of Strategic Services (World War II forerunner of the CIA), was also said to stand for "Oh So Social" because of the number of Ivy League recruits in its ranks.

The eight Ivy League colleges may be recalled by using the first letter of each word in the sentence—

Preppy Premeds Can't Hack College, Yet Drink Beer.

D. Jaffe, Ithaca, N.Y.

P — Princeton
P — Penn
C — Cornell
H — Harvard
C — Columbia
Y — Yale
D — Dartmouth
B — Brown

Here's a good technique for studying (easy to remember because the letters are in order) —

P Q R S T

P — Preview
Q — Question
R — Read
S — State
T — Test

And an alternative technique which is more widely used—

SQ3R

S — Survey
Q — Question
R — Read
R — Recite
R — Review

How to remember what the sixteenth to the nineteenth amendments to the U.S. Constitution are concerned with (in order) —

In come the senators with wine and women.

In come	— 16th Amendment —	Established Income Tax
senators	— 17th Amendment —	Direct Election of U.S. Senators
wine	— 18th Amendment —	Prohibition
women	— 19th Amendment —	Women's Suffrage

You will probably never see this on a history test, but it's far more important in the long run. The potential murder weapons in the game of Clue (in case you lose your score sheet)—

Kangaroos **R**espond **W**hen **L**emmings
Run **C**ounterclockwise.

K — Knife
R — Revolver
W — Wrench
L — Lead pipe
R — Rope
C — Candlestick

The Seven Wonders of the Ancient World can be remembered by visualizing a crack in the earth which is destroying all but the pyramids—

CAZM GAP

C — Colossus of Rhodes	(Statue over 100 ft. tall)
A — Artemis, Temple of—at Ephesus	(Famous for its size and art)
Z — Zeus, Statue of—at Olympia	(Covered with gold and ivory)
M — Mausoleum of Hapicarnassus	(Fragments in British Museum)
G — Gardens of Babylon, Hanging	(Built by Nebuchadrezzar)
A — Alexandria, Pharos of	(Famous ancient lighthouse)
P — Pyramids of Egypt	(The only survivor)

How to remember which ear a Hawaiian girl wears a flower over to mean she's "taken"—

The left ear—same as the left hand for the wedding band

A flower over the right ear means she's looking.

Keeping the ears straight could be very important!

The information that a policeman radios back to headquarters about a motor vehicle (in the recommended order)—

CYMBOL

C — Color
Y — Year
M — Make
B — Body style

O —Occupants
L —License plate no.

The musical instrument is spelled cymbal, of course.

How to remember the persons whose portraits appear on U.S. paper money, past and present, in order of increasing value—

When Jack Lemmon Handed Joel Grey Five Movie Contracts, Many Critics Whined.

Anthony Osinski, Canonsburg, Pa.

W — Washington—$1
J — Jefferson—$2
L — Lincoln—$5
H — Hamilton—$10
J — Jackson—$20
G — Grant—$50
F — Franklin—$100
M — McKinley—$500
C — Cleveland—$1000
M — Madison—$5000
C — Chase—$10,000
W — Wilson—$100,000

Jewelers use these key elements in evaluating diamonds—

The Four C's

Color
Cut
Carat weight
Clarity

A way to remember how much a carat weighs—it's five letters long and it equals ⅕ of a gram.

See Chapter 5 on Aviation for the four C's to remember in a general aviation emergency and Chapter 12 on Business for Thomas Watson's five C's (Data Processing section).

There are at least two sentences that will help you remember the ten major categories of the Dewey Decimal System (the traditional method of categorizing library books) —

General, File Religiously, So Languidly, Scientifically.
Treat Art Like History.

or

Good Pupils Require Speedy Learning;
So Use Fine Library Helpers.

Mark Pellegrino, Rocky Point, N.Y.

000 — General Works
100 — Philosophy
200 — Religion
300 — Social Sciences
400 — Language
500 — Science (Pure)
600 — Technology (Useful Arts, Applied Science)
700 — The Fine Arts
800 — Literature
900 — History

There is a recommended sequence for listing illustration details in a book (not that of the 1967 Library Association code). The collation catalogue entry for the book is in this order—

Flirting Ill-Pleases Parents Pursuing
Matrimonial Plans For Their Daughters.

F — Frontispiece
I — Illustrations
P — Plates
P — Photographs
P — Portraits
M — Maps
P — Plans
F — Facsimiles
T — Tables
D — Diagrams

If you've never been able to keep all those lords and ladies in British novels straight, here's the order of degree of British hereditary titles in descending sequence of importance—

Did Mary Ever Visit Brighton Beach?

D — Duke
M — Marquis
E — Earl
V — Viscount

B — Baron
B — Baronet

There are two equally appropriate explanations of how teen-agers interpret a **STOP** sign—

S — Slight		S — Squeal
T — Tap	or	T — Tires
O — On		O — On
P — Pedal		P — Pavement

A general rule for Boy Scout projects, which the Pentagon would do well to observe—

KISMIF

K — Keep
I — It
S — Simple
M — Make
I — It
F — Fun

Another scouting mnemonic (also used in the navy) helps you to remember how to tie a bowline knot (as the rope follows the path of the rabbit)—

> The rabbit comes out of the hole,
> goes around the tree, and back in the hole.

The "tree" may be the standing line.

A simpler and more common knot—the square knot—may be tied by remembering this phrase—

> Right over left, then left over right.

Samuel F.B. Morse invented the code that bears his name in 1837. Generations of servicemen and Boy Scouts have memorized the code, mostly by rote. The following is a set of mnemonic devices for remembering the allocation of Morse code dots and dashes (also called dits and das) for the letters of the alphabet (dots are short syllables and dashes are long syllables)—

A .–   Alone
B –...   Beautifully
C –.–.   Correspondent

D –.. Daintily
E – Egg
F ..–. For a fortnight
G ––. Good gracious
H .... Ha ha ha ha
I .. Is it?
J .––– Japan's jam jars
K –.– Kiss me Kate
L .–.. Linoleum
M –– Moonshine
N –. Naughty
O ––– Our old oak
P .––. Polite person
Q ––.– Quite queer & quaint
R .–. Rewarding
S ... Sisterly
T – Tea
U ..– Underneath
V ...– Very verbose
W .–– Without waste
X –..– Extra expense
Y –.–– Yellow yacht's yarn
Z ––.. Zoological

The international distress signal SOS is a form of mnemonic in that it was chosen because in Morse code it is simply *dot dot dot, dash dash dash, dot dot dot*—easy to remember, transmit, receive, and recognize. It does not stand for 'Save our ship' or any other combination of words.

Advice on how to screw—

Right is tight. (Clockwise, that is.)

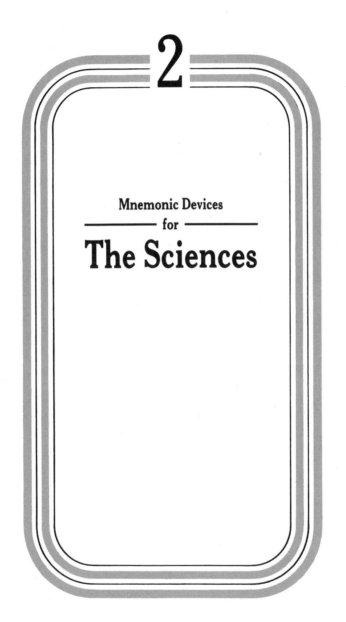

2

Mnemonic Devices
— for —
The Sciences

The various fields of science have been very fertile ground for mnemonic devices since so much memorization is required to master these disciplines. One of the most commonly used devices is for the order of the planets going out from the sun. Mathematics, which obviously involves numbers, uses several devices (especially to remember pi to several decimal places) where you count the number of letters in each word of the sentence or poem.

Memory aids for calendars, time, and the seasons have been grouped together as one section because of the overlapping nature of these subjects. There are separate chapters for Medicine/Psychology and Geography/Travel because there are so many examples in these fields.

The Scientific Method is the way that researchers go about investigating their various fields of study. By using this method correctly, others will be able to follow the process, duplicate the experiments and arrive at the same conclusions. It is the basis of all scientific study and discovery.

**The Purple Hippopotamus Marches
Proudly Down Central Safely.**

T — Thesis
P — Proposition
H — Hypothesis
M — Materials
P — Procedure
D — Data
C — Conclusions
S — Summary

The metric system of measures (in descending order) may be remembered with either—

Kippers Hardly Dare Move During Cold Months.

or

King Henry Dies Merrily During Christmas Mass.

K — Kilometer
H — Heclometer
D — Dekameter
M — Meter
D — Decimeter
C — Centimeter
M — Millimeter

Another sentence for the metric prefixes of decreasing quantity starting at one tenth—

Damn **C**lever **M**nemonic **M**akes **N**o **P**refix **F**orgettable.

Larry Johnson, Boston, Mass.

D — deci	10 to the -1st	"one tenth"
C — centi	10 to the -2nd	"one hundredth"
M — milli	10 to the -3rd	"one thousandth"
M — micro	10 to the -6th	"one millionth"
N — nano	10 to the -9th	"one billionth"
P — pico	10 to the -12th	"one trillionth"
F — femto	10 to the -15th	"one quadrillionth"

The numeric value for the temperature of absolute zero (counting the number of letters in each word)—

Soon super soporific stupor spreads.
—459.67 degrees Fahrenheit

The chief constituents of soil—

All **H**airy **M**en **W**ill **B**uy **R**azors.

A — Air
H — Humus
M — Mineral salts
W — Water
B — Bacteria
R — Rock particles

The stages in mitosis and meiosis, the types of cell division—

Mitosis—**P**eas **M**ake **A**wful **T**arts.

P — Prophase
M — Metaphase
A — Anaphase
T — Telophase

Meiosis—**L**azy **Z**ulus **P**ursue **D**ark **D**amsels.

L — Lepotene
Z — Zygotene
P — Pachytene
D — Diplotene
D — Diakinesis

You can remember the general categories of trees by using the letters "D" and "C"—

Deciduous trees **D**rop their leaves, **C**onifers bear **C**ones.

Astronomy

The order of classes in the spectral sequence of stars (from the hottest class stars to the coolest). This mnemonic was devised by one of two astronomers—either Henry Norris Russell or George Gamow—

Oh Be A Fine Girl Kiss Me.

Class		Color	Degrees (Kelvin)
O	— Hottest stars	— Blue	— > 25,000
B		— Blue	— 11,000 to 25,000
A		— Blue	— 7,500 to 11,000
F		— Blue to White	— 6,000 to 7,500
G		— White to Yellow	— 5,000 to 6,000
K		— Orange to Red	— 3,500 to 5,000
M	— Coolest Stars	— Red	— < 3,500

There are three rare classes of stars cooler than M that may be added to the above. They are R, N, and S class stars and may be remembered by adding **R**ight **N**ow **S**weetheart on to the phrase above.

The five brightest stars (in descending order)—

Stars Can ACtually Aid Vision.

S   — Sirius
C   — Canopus
AC — Alpha Centauri
A   — Arcturus
V   — Vega

Alpha Centauri is 30 degrees north of the south celestial pole and can only be seen from the southern hemisphere.

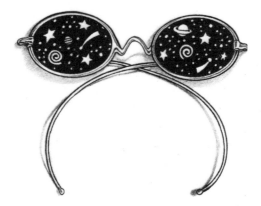

The five closest stars (in order starting with the nearest)—
Always **B**e **W**ary **L**ocating **S**tars.

A — Alpha Centauri (4.27 light years away)
B — Barnard's Star (5.97 light years away)
W — Wolf 359 (7.66 light years away)
L — Lalande 21185 (8.12 light years away)
S — Sirius (8.70 light years away)

Sirius is the nearest star that can be seen with the naked eye from most of the United States.

There are many different sentences used to remember the planets of our solar system (in sequence from the Sun out) including the asteroid belt, which is probably the remnants of a planet. The one I like best involves some U.S. presidents—
Martin **V**an Buren **E**ats **M**rs. **A**dams' **J**elly **S**andwich **U**nder **N**ixon's **P**orch.

M — Mercury
V — Venus
E — Earth
M — Mars
A — Asteroid belt
J — Jupiter
S — Saturn
U — Uranus
N — Neptune
P — Pluto

Some of the better known mnemonic devices for the planets leave out the asteroid belt—

Men **V**ery **E**asily **M**ake **J**ugs **S**erve **U**seful
Nocturnal **P**urposes.

or

My **V**ery **E**arnest **M**other **J**ust **S**ent **U**s
Nine **P**ickles.

or

Mary's **V**iolet **E**yes **M**ake **J**ohn **S**tay **U**p
Nights **P**acing.

All of these devices are temporarily inaccurate since Pluto will be closer to the sun than Neptune for the next several years because of the nature of its elliptical orbit. The search for a tenth planet has also recently been accelerated.

Here are the nine planets, in order of increasing size—

Men **P**lan **M**any **VENUS** **J**umps.

Jim Wildermuth, Riverside, Calif.

M — Mercury
P — Pluto
M — Mars
V — Venus
E — Earth
N — Neptune
U — Uranus
S — Saturn
J — Jupiter

Here's a good way to remember the discoverer of the planet Pluto (on 3/13/30) by using the name of the planet itself—

The first two letters, and the astronomical symbol, of the planet Pluto are his initials—**Percival Lowell**

How to distinguish between the phases of waxing and waning of the earth's moon—

If the moon's crescent fits the natural curve of the right hand (backwards C) then it is *Increasing* or *waxing* (the word "right" contains an "I"). If the curve of the left hand fits (C) then it is *dEcreasing* or *waning* (the word "left" contains an "E").

or, in Latin—

Luna mentitur, quia quando dicit
Se crescere, decrescit, et quando dicit
Se decrescere, crescit.

which, translated, says:

Thou art not crescent when a C,
Nor yet decrescent when a D.

The two moons of Mars, from the planet out (both are very small)—

Pretty **D**iminutive

P — Phobos
D — Deimos

The ten named moons of Saturn, from the planet out—

Jade **M**oons **E**ncircle **T**hat **D**elightful **R**inged **T**itan, **H**eeding **I**ts **P**ower.

Ernest Sciaroni, St. Louis, Mo.

J — Janus
M — Mimas
E — Enceladus
T — Tethys
D — Dione
R — Rhea
T — Titan
H — Hyperion
I — Iapetus
P — Phoebe

The five large (and therefore named) moons of Uranus, from the planet out—

M-AUTO

M — Miranda
A — Ariel
U — Umbriel
T — Titania
O — Oberon

The four largest asteroids (not to be confused with the video game)—

Certain Photos Verify Juno.

C — Ceres (785 km. in diameter)
P — Pallas (489 km. in diameter)
V — Vesta (399 km. in diameter)
J — Juno (190 km. in diameter)

Biology

You can use an image of a king striding over a map to remember the method of classifying flora and fauna; the sequence of taxonomic classification—

King Philip Conquers Over Fifty Grateful States.

K — Kingdom
P — Phylum
C — Class
O — Order
F — Family
G — Genus
S — Species

Two alternatives are:

**Krakatoa Positively Casts Off Fumes
Generating Sulphurous Vapors.**

or

Kindly Place Covers On Fresh Green Spicy Vegetables.

where the V stands for Variety, a subdivision of species.

A British-created memory aid for the major characteristics of living organisms (Newmarket is the location of a well-known English horse race)—

Newmarket Runs Every Great Race In May.

N — Nutrition
R — Respiration
E — Excretion
G — Growth
R — Reproduction
I — Irritability (response to conditions)
M — Movement

The biological classification of man may be remembered by—
> **A**ll **C**haperones **M**ust **P**reviously **H**ave **H**ad **S**ex.
>   *Greg Freeman, Newnan, Ga.*

A — Animalia
C — Chordata
M — Mammalia
P — Primate
H — Hominidae
H — Homo
S — Sapiens

Calendar, Time, and Seasons

In 46 B.C., Julius Caesar authorized the calendar with every fourth year containing an extra day. Catholic countries adopted the Gregorian calendar by papal decree in 1582, but England, by then a non-Catholic country, remained on the Julian calendar until 1752.

The largest periods of times are the eras—
> **C**areful **M**en **P**ay **E**asily.

C — Cenozoic—70 million years ago to present
M — Mesozoic—200 million years ago to 70 million years ago
P — Paleozoic—620 million years ago to 200 million years ago
E — Eozoic—Greater than 620 million years ago

Many people remember the number of days in the months of the year with this poem—

> Thirty days hath September,
> April, June, and November
> All the rest have Thirty-One,
> Save for February alone.
> Which has but twenty-eight in fine
> Till leap year gives it twenty-nine.

Another way to remember the above is by using your fist (assuming you have all your knuckles). Start by naming the knuckle of your index finger as "January", the valley between it and the next finger as "February", the middle finger knuckle as "March", etc., until you get to the little finger knuckle which will be "July". Then you come back by touching the little finger knuckle a second time and naming it "August", the next valley "September", and finally ending up on the middle finger knuckle with "December". All knuckles represent 31-day months and all valleys represent non-31-day months.

> Leap year is given, when 4 will divide,
> The cent'ries complete, or odd years beside.

(1988/4 = 497 with no remainder, therefore it is a leap year.

1900 is a century year so 19/4 = 4 with a remainder of 3, so it is not a leap year, but 2000 will be.)

When is Easter?

> No need for confusion if we but recall
> That Easter on the first Sunday after the full moon
> Following the vernal equinox doth fall.
> > *Justin Richardson (1899–)*

How to set your clocks going on and off Daylight Savings Time—
Spring Ahead, Fall Back

which means set your clock ahead one hour in the spring, and back one hour in the fall.

The astrological year begins with Aries, the Ram. The following is a poem to remember the signs of the Zodiac in sequence—

> Our vernal signs the **RAM** begins,
> Then comes the **BULL**, in May the **TWINS**;
> The **CRAB** in June, next **LEO** shines,
> And **VIRGO** ends the northern signs.
> The **BALANCE** brings autumnal fruits,
> The **SCORPION** stings, the **ARCHER** shoots;
> December's **GOAT** brings wintry blast;
> **AQUARIUS** rain, the **FISH** comes last.
> > *Ebenezer Cobham Brewer (1810–1897)*

A sentence to remember the Zodiacal signs in order—
As **T**he **G**reat **C**ook **L**ikes **V**ery **L**ittle **S**alt
She **C**ompensates **A**dding **P**epper.

A — Aries
T — Taurus
G — Gemini
C — Cancer
L — Leo

V — Virgo
L — Libra
S — Scorpio
S — Sagittarius
C — Capricorn
A — Aquarius
P — Pisces

Chemistry

With over 100 elements in the periodic table and a vast number of other facts that a chemist should commit to memory, it is small wonder that there are many chemical mnemonic devices.

The symbols for the elements in Atomic Number sequence (from 1 through 20) may be remembered with the sentence below. The Atomic Number represents the number of protons in the nucleus which in a neutral atom equals the number of electrons outside the nucleus. This number determines the place of the element in the periodic table.

**Hydrogen, His Little Bells Bonging Carl,
Nudged Over Four New Nags Making Al See
Present Situation Clearly And Karen Collaborated.**

Atomic No.	Symbol	Phosphorus
1	H	Hydrogen
2	He	Helium
3	Li	Lithium
4	Be	Beryllium
5	B	Boron
6	C	Carbon
7	N	Nitrogen
8	O	Oxygen
9	F	Fluorine
10	Ne	Neon
11	Na	Sodium
12	Mg	Magnesium
13	Al	Aluminum
14	Si	Silicon
15	P	Phosphorus
16	S	Sulfur
17	Cl	Chlorine
18	Ar	Argon
19	K	Potassium
20	Ca	Calcium

The symbols for the elements in Atomic Number sequence (from 2 through 19) may be remembered with the three sentences below. These three sentences make more sense to most people than the one above.

Here **Li**es **Be**njamin **B**old.
Cry **N**ot **O**ld **F**riend **N**eedlessly.
Nature **Mg**nifies **Al**l **Si**mple **P**eople,
Sometimes **Cl**ods **Ar**e **K**ings.

For elements Na—Ar (numbers 11 through 18)—
Nagging **Mag**gie **Al**ways **SiPS ClAr**et.

Na — Sodium
Mg — Magnesium
Al   — Aluminum
Si   — Silicon
P   — Phosphorus
S   — Sulfur
Cl   — Chlorine
Ar — Argon

For elements Cs—Re (numbers 55–57 and 72–75, omitting the Lathanides)—
Cows **B**ear **La**rger **H**eifers **T**han **W**e **Re**alize.

Cs — Cesium
Ba — Barium
La — Lanthanum
Hf — Hafnium
Ta — Tantalum
W   — Tungsten
Re — Rhenium

For elements Au—Po (numbers 79 through 84)—
Audacious **Hg**s s**T**ealing, wee**P** because of **Bi**tter **Po**verty.

Au — Gold
Hg — Mercury
Tl   — Thallium
Pb — Lead
Bi   — Bismuth
Po — Polonium

For elements Th—Md (numbers 90 through 101)—

Though **P**arsons **U**se **N**apkins **P**uny **Am**ericans
Consu**m**e **B**lack **C**off**eEs F**rom **M**aids.

Th — Thorium
Pa — Protactinium
U   — Uranium
Np — Neptunium
Pu — Plutonium
Am — Americium
Cm — Curium
Bk — Berkelium
Cf — Californium
Es — Einsteinium
Fm — Fermium
Md — Mendelevium

For elements 86 to 101—

Ren**o**unce, **F**rust**R**ated **A**lchemist,
This **P**atently **UN**po**Pu**lar **A**tomic **C**onundrum!
Bloc**k**heads **C**an't **f**ind **E**lement**s**
From **M**nemonic **d**evices.

Rn — Radon
Fr — Francium
Ra — Radium
Ac — Actinium
Th — Thorium
Pa — Protactinium
U   — Uranium
Np — Neptunium
Pu — Plutonium
Am — Americium
Cm — Curium
Bk — Berkelium
Cf — Californium
Es — Einsteinium
Fm — Fermium
Md — Mendelevium

The four essential elements that are the basic building blocks of life—

No Help On Creation.

N   — Nitrogen
H   — Hydrogen
O   — Oxygen
C   — Carbon

The four nitrogen bases of DNA, by linkage pairs—

A True Genetic Chain.

Don Hagen, Eureka, Calif.

A — Adenine
T — Thymine
G — Guanine
C — Cytosine

Rules for Solubility (the ability to dissolve), an important characteristic in chemistry—

> Potassium, sodium and ammonium salts
> Whatever they may be,
> Can always be depended on
> For solubility.

> When asked about the nitrates,
> The answer's always clear,
> "They each and all are soluble,"
> Is all we want to hear.

> Most every chloride's soluble
> At least we've always read,
> Save silver, mercurous mercury
> And (slightly) chloride of lead.

> Every single sulfate
> Is soluble, 'Tis said,
> 'Cept barium and strontium
> And calcium and lead.

> Hydroxides of metals won't dissolve,
> That is, all but three,
> Potassium, sodium and ammonium,
> Dissolve quite readily.

> And then you must remember
> That you must not "forgit"

Calcium, barium and strontium
Dissolve a little bit.

The carbonates, insoluble,
It's lucky that it's so,
Or else, our marble buildings
Would melt away like snow.

(Repeat, with feeling)

Potassium, sodium and ammonium salts
Whatever they may be,
Can always be depended on
For solubility.

From Cornell University

For the rare inert gases (group O) —
   Heaven **Ne**ver **A**sked **Kr**iegspiel's **Ex**tra **R**ent.

He — Helium
Ne — Neon
A — Argon
Kr — Krypton
Ex — Xenon
Rn — Radon

Electronics

There are many versions of sentences to remember the resistor color codes (in order by their numerical equivalent). One slightly sanitized version goes "Bad boys ravage our young girls behind victory garden walls." After World War II, the phrase "victory gardens" became obsolete so the final four words were changed to ". . . but Violet gives willingly." The following sentence is a bit tamer—

   Bad **B**ooze **R**ots **O**ur **Y**oung **G**uts **B**ut **V**odka **G**oes **W**ell.

B — Black — 1
B — Brown — 2
R — Red   — 3
O — Orange — 4
Y — Yellow — 5
G — Green — 6
B — Blue   — 7
V — Violet — 8
G — Gray   — 9
W — White — 0

Always three colors with the third indicating the number of zeros after the the first two digits (e.g., 1900 Ohms of resistance would be represented by black, gray, and brown stripes near the end of a resistor).

Silver or gold stripes mean the rating may vary by plus or minus 10 or 5 percent.

One of the most fundamental rules of electricity is Ohm's law—
Virgins **A**re **R**are.

Volts = Amps X Resistance

To remember which leads which in inductance and capacitor circuits—
ELI the **ICE** man
where E = Voltage
　　　　L = Inductance
　　　　I = Current
　　　　C = Capacitor

In other words, Voltage leads Current in an Inductance circuit and Current leads Voltage in a Capacitor circuit.

Using the same symbols as the above example, you can remember the definition of Power with—
PIE

Power = Current X Voltage

For converters and inverters—
CAD and **IDA**
CAD — **C**onverters change **A**C to **D**C.
IDA — **I**nverters change **D**C to **A**C.

There are three basic formats for videotape used throughout the world. Most of Europe uses PAL format (Phase Alternating Lines) but France uses SECAM. The United States uses NTSC (National Television Standards Committee) which Europeans can remember with the phrase—
Not **T**he **S**ame **C**olor

because an NTSC videotape does not display the correct colors when played on a European VCR.

Geology

All known history is divided into geological time periods which may be remembered with three sentences (in order, from the earliest to the most current age) —

Camels Often Sit Down Carefully.
Perhaps Their Joints Creak?
Early Oiling Might Prevent Permanent Rheumatism.

C	— Cambrian	— Invertebrates flourish
O	— Ordovician	— First fish, vertebrates
S	— Silurian	— First vascular plants, land animals
D	— Devonian	— First insects, amphibians
C	— Carboniferous	— First trees, reptiles
P	— Permian	— First dinosaurs, conifers
T	— Triassic	— First mammals
J	— Jurassic	— First birds, dinosaurs' zenith
C	— Cretaceous	— First flowers, extinction of dinosaurs
E	— Eocene	— Rise of flowering plants
O	— Oligocene	— First large browsing mammals
M	— Miocene	— First whales, apes, grazing forms
P	— Pliocene	— First humans
P	— Pleistocene	— Great Ice Age
R	— Recent	— First book on mnemonics

The names of the periods in the Paleozoic era (with the Carboniferous era divided into the Mississippian and Pennsylvanian eras) —

Can Oscar See Down My Pants Pocket?

C	— Cambrian
O	— Ordovician
S	— Silurian
D	— Devonian
M	— Mississippian
P	— Pennsylvanian
P	— Permian

The Great Ice Age, also known as the Pleistocene Epoch, had four great periods of glaciation in North America. The names of these glacial periods all originate in the upper Mississippi valley where those types of areas or sections occur. They may be remembered, from earliest to latest, with the sentence—

Never Kiss Indian Women.

N — Nebraskan glacial period
       Aftonian interglacial   — A
K — Kansan glacial period
       Yarmouth interglacial — Y
I — Illinois glacial period
       Sangamon interglacial— S
W — Wisconsin glacial period

The interglacial periods (above, in the same order) may be remembered with a phrase that would seem to logically follow—

Angry Young Squaws

The most abundant elements in the earth's crust, in sequence by the percent of total weight—

Only Silly Asses In College Study Past Midnight.

O — Oxygen   — 46.6%
S — Silicon   — 27.7%
A — Aluminum   — 8.1%
I — Iron   — 5.0%
C — Calcium   — 3.6%
S — Sodium   — 2.8%
P — Potassium — 2.6%
M — Magnesium — 2.1%

While oxygen is 46.6% of the earth's crust by weight, it is almost exactly double that (93.8%) by volume.

The Mohs scale of mineral hardness, determined by its resistance to scratching by one of the following minerals (softest to hardest)—

The Girls Could Flirt And Other Queer Things Could Do.

T — Talc
G — Gypsum
C — Calcite
F — Fluorite
A — Apatite
O — Orthoclase
Q — Quartz
T — Topaz
C — Corundum
D — Diamond

An alternative sentence which is more difficult to remember but has the advantage of the first two letters of each word matching the first two letters of each metal—

Tall **Gy**roscopes **Ca**n **Fl**y **Ap**art **Or**biting **Qu**ickly **To** **Co**mplete **Di**sintegration.

Another sentence which may be used if you want to remember Feldspar instead of Orthoclase—

Tall **Gy**psies **Ca**n **F**urnish **A**t **F**risco
Quite **T**empting **C**an-**C**an **D**ances.

This scale was devised by Friedrich Mohs (1773–1839), a German mineralogist.

How to remember the difference between stalagmites and stalactites: look at the first letter that is different—the sixth letter.

g — up from the **G**round
c — down from the **C**eiling
or
The mites go up and the tites come down.

Horticulture

Here is a cheer that you can use to remember the five symptoms of bacterial disease in plants—

Root rot, leaf spot,
Blight, Wilt, Gall.
Ask me again and I'll
Tell you them all.
Cindy Henderson, Plano, Texas

The 16 essential elements for plant growth may be recalled with the following—

See Hopkins cafe managed by mine cousin Mo Clancy.

See	— C	Carbon
Hopkins	— H O P K N S	Hydrogen, Oxygen, Phosphorus, Potassium, Nitrogen, Sulfur
Cafe	— Ca Fe	Calcium, Iron
managed	— Mg	Magnesium
by	— B	Boron
mine	— Mn	Manganese
cousin	— Cu Zn	Copper, Zinc
Mo	— Mo	Molybdenum
Clancy	— Cl	Chlorine

The gardener's rule applies to youth and age: When young "sow wild oats," but when old "grow sage."

Mathematics

Believe it or not, there is a clever mnemonic device, created by Daniel Gilbert, for remembering the first ten integers (whole numbers). So for those who have trouble counting from 1 to 10—

Only **T**he **T**ruly **F**orgetful **F**ellow **S**hould
Summon **E**ach **N**umber **T**husly.

There are several ways of remembering how to calculate the trigonometric functions. The best known one involves a mental picture of a King soaking his toe (King **SOH CAH TOA**) but the unusual spelling leads to errors. The following is a sentence that uses the same letters and is probably easier to remember—

Sir **O**liver's **H**orse **C**ame **A**mbling **H**ome
To **O**liver's **A**unt.

or

Some **O**fficers **H**ave **C**urly **A**uburn **H**air
To **O**ffer **A**ttraction.

Sine = **O**pposite / **H**ypotenuse
Cosine = **A**djacent / **H**ypotenuse
Tangent = **O**pposite / **A**djacent

Another sentence which places the tangent first is—

Tall **O**striches **A**re **S**cared **O**f
Huge **C**rocodiles **A**nd **H**ippos.

Yet another sentence that involves a pattern of placing the first three words over the last three—

Oscar	**A**nd	**O**liver
Have	**H**ad	**A**lgebra.
(Sine)	(Cosine)	(Tangent)

To remember which trigonometric functions are positive in which graph quadrants—

All **S**tudents **T**ake **C**alculus.

All — All functions are positive in the first quadrant
S — Sine and cosecant positive in the second quadrant
T — Tangent and cotangent positive in the third quadrant
C — Cosine and secant positive in the fourth quadrant

A sentence to remember the above in the same sequence—
All Sinful **C**ompany **S**upervisors
Cavort on **Tan Cot**s with **C**ozy **Sec**retaries.

The most common way of remembering pi (an irrational number representing the circumference of a circle divided by the diameter) is to use the fraction $^{22}/_7$ which equals 3.14, carried to two decimal places, but the following sentence helps you remember it to six places—

How I wish I could calculate "pie"
(use the number of letters in each word—3.141593)

Another sentence which takes pi to 14 decimal places—

Now I want a drink, alcoholic of course,
after the heavy chapters involving quantum mechanics.
(3.14159265358979)

There is a fraction that is as easily remembered as $^{22}/_7$ which uses the first three odd numbers, 113 under 355, which equals 3.141593. (Notice that the last 3 digits of the fraction are the numerator.)

To remember pi to thirty decimal places, again using the number of letters in each word (from the *Mensa Journal*)—

Sir, I send a rhyme excelling
In sacred truth and rigid spelling.
Numerical sprites elucidate,
All my own striving can't relate.
If nature gain,
Not you complain,
Though Doctor Johnson fulminate.

(3.141592653589793238462643386679)

There are similar rhymes for the square roots of two, three, and five—

The square root of two (1.414)—

I wish I knew (the root of two)

or to ten decimal places—

I have a root of a two
whose square is two (1.4142135623).

The square root of three (1.732)—

O charmed was he (to know the root of three)

The square root of five (2.236)—

So we now strive (to find the root of five)

Avogadro's number, which is the number of molecules in a mole of a substance (6.023 X 10 to the 23rd) —

> Number, constantly in use (in the laboratory)
> *Douglas R. Frank, Great Lakes, Ill.*

Avogadro's law is the principle that equal volumes of different gases under identical conditions of pressure and temperature contain the same number of molecules.

The difference between the ordinate and abscissa (in a plane Cartesian coordinate system) —

> You can put a "pizza" on the abscissa.

The abscissa is the horizontal distance from the y-axis to the point, whereas the ordinate is the vertical distance from the x-axis to the point.

How to multiply expressions with parentheses in Algebra—

FOIL

F — First
O — Outside
I — Inside
L — Last

Rule for the sequence of mathematical operations—

> **P**lease **E**xcuse **M**y **D**ear **A**unt **S**ally.

P — Parentheses
E — Exponentiation
M — Multiplication
D — Division
A — Addition
S — Subtraction

"Bless" may be substituted for "Please" if Brackets are to be remembered instead of Parentheses.

Roman Numerals — X shall stand for playmates ten
V for five stout stalwart men
I for one as I'm alive
C for hundred, D for five (hundred)
M for a thousand soldiers true, and
L for 50, I'll tell you.

Garrison Keillor's school had MCMII etched in the cornerstone of the building, which he interpreted to mean "Middle Child

Means Incredible Intelligence," since he was the middle child of his family.

A sentence to remember the numerals in ascending order—
   In Various Xmas Legends, Christ Delivers Miracles.
                                        David Furbush, Las Vegas, Nev.

I — One
V — Five
X — Ten
L — Fifty
C — One Hundred
D — Five Hundred
M — One Thousand

On the divisibility of numbers—

> Here are memory methods by which to decide,
> By glancing at numbers, the way they'll divide.
> When the unit is even, you quickly will see,
> The whole of the number by 2 cut can be.
> When the unit is either a naught or a 5,
> A slash with a 5 you throughout can contrive.
> Any figures whatever you'll easily trace
> By 2 and 5 cut, when beyond unit's place.
> If the last two by 4 are divisible, see,
> The whole line by 4 will divisible be.
> When you find the last 3 can be cut by an 8,
> 8 will cut through them all, you may fearlessly state.
> Cut the sum of the digits by 9 or by 3,
> And in similar manner the number will be.
> A number that's even, and by 3 divides,
> Can always by 6 be divided besides.
> When a number will cut up by 4 and 3, note,
> It divides too by 12, you for certain can quote.
> Whenever your digits alternately take,
> And the sum of the series from other will make,
> 11 or naught as a remainder, decide
> You can by 11 that number divide.
> It is only when 0 is the last figure seen,
> That the series by 10 could divided have been.
> For dividing by 7 no rule will apply,
> If you doubt the assertion, to find a rule try.
>   *William Stokes*

Optics

The colors of the visible spectrum (in sequence by wave length) —

Roy G. Biv
In England they use **R**ichard **O**f **Y**ork
Gave **B**attles **I**n **V**ain
or
Roll **O**ut **Y**our **G**uiness **B**oys, **I**n **V**ats.

R — Red
O — Orange
Y — Yellow
G — Green
B — Blue
I — Indigo
V — Violet

The additive and subtractive mixtures of colors—

Better **G**et **R**eady **W**hile
Your **M**istress **C**omes **B**ack.

Blue + Green + Red = White (additive)
Yellow + Magenta + Cyan = Black (subtractive)

The color wheel as used in photography—

Rich **Y**oung **G**irls **C**an **B**e **M**ade.

R — Red
Y — Yellow
G — Green
C — Cyan
B — Blue
M — Magenta

Weather

Everyone talks about it, and most people use memory aids to help predict or understand the weather.

The layers of the earth's atmosphere, from lowest to highest—

This **S**ystem **M**akes **I**t **E**asy.

Ann Marie Perun, Toronto, Ohio

T — Troposphere
S — Stratosphere
M — Mesosphere
I — Ionosphere
E — Exosphere

An approximate range of Centigrade temperatures—

> 30° is hot,
> 20° is nice,
> 10° is cool, and
> 0° is ice

30° Centigrade = 86° Fahrenheit
20°   = 68°
10°   = 50°
 0°   = 32°

The formula for converting Fahrenheit to Celsius may be remembered with this sentence—

> Celsius equals foolish nonsense because
> Fahrenheit makes temperature the best.

which corresponds to the formula (in words)—

> Celsius equals five-ninths bracket
> Fahrenheit minus thirty-two bracket

or in symbols—

$$C = \tfrac{5}{9} (F - 32)$$

e.g., to convert 50 degrees Fahrenheit to Celsius

$$C = \tfrac{5}{9} (50 - 32)$$
$$C = \tfrac{5}{9} (18)$$
$$C = 10°$$

Here are a few words of weather wisdom—

> Evening red, morning gray,
> Sends the traveler on his way.
> Evening gray, morning red,
> Brings down rain upon his head.
>
> Mackerel sky and mare's tails
> Make tall ships carry small sails.

Using the moon to predict weather at sea (also commonly remembered with "Red sky" substituted for "Halo")—

> Halo in the morning, sailor take warning.
> Halo at night, sailor's delight.

How to remember the direction of the winds around a high pressure area (low pressure being the opposite)—

High Noon

(The word Noon referring to a clock—winds go clockwise around a "High" pressure area.)

Also, water spins counterclockwise down the drain in the northern hemisphere, which can be remembered by comparing it to a low pressure area—the water is going to a lower place.

Another way to locate low pressure areas: stand with your back to the wind—the Low pressure area is on your Left.

> Rain on Good Friday and Easter Day,
> A good year for grass and a bad year for hay.

Zoology

The six groups of purebred dogs—

Some Hounds Wag Their Tails Nonstop.

Terry McNamee, Stoney Creek, Ontario, Canada

S — Sporting
H — Hound
W — Working
T — Terrier
T — Toy
N — Nonsporting

A zoological ditty—

Ontogeny recapitulates Phylogeny.

which means that the history of the individual retraces the history of the race. This explains why human fetuses have gill slits and tails at various stages of development.

The parts of an insect's leg—

Cockroaches Travel Fast Towards Their Children.

C — Coxa
T — Trochanter
F — Femur
T — Tibia
T — Tarsus
C — Claw

The order in which the arteries in a frog branch off the main aorta—

Little **M**en **I**n **S**hort **B**lack **M**ackintoshes.

A. English, London, England

L — Lingual
M — Mandibular
I — Innominate
S — Subclavian
B — Brachial
M — Musculocutaneous

How to remember the differences between similar animals—

Elephants — the shape of their ears matches the shape of their locales. African elephants have large, bulging ears, similar to the African continent; Indian elephants have smaller, more triangular ears, similar to the shape of India.

Alligators/Crocodiles — Alligators have a wide, blunt nose somewhat like an "alley"; crocodiles have a narrow pointed nose somewhat like a sun "dial."

Camels — Arabian camels have a single hump — A is letter 1. Bactrian camels have two humps — B is letter 2.

> The camel has a single hump,
> The dromedary two.
> Or else the other way around,
> I'm never sure, are you?
>
> *Ogden Nash*

(It's the other way around. The word "dromedary" comes from the Greek word "dromos" meaning "race-course"; therefore, dromedaries are the racing camels.)

> A camel I am it's plain to see
> But am I a Bactrian or a Dromedary?
> Lay down the B and then the D
> And which I am is plain as can be.

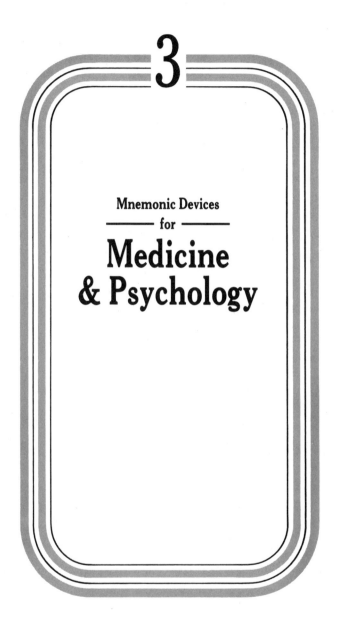

3

Mnemonic Devices
— for —
Medicine
& Psychology

The medical field probably has more memory aids than any other single field of study. Doctors are expected to know thousands of anatomical facts as well as the manner in which different parts of the body function. Doctors also seem to have a rather lusty sense of humor because many of these examples are somewhat bawdy. The mnemonic devices used by the medical field have changed over the years because, in some cases, anatomists have changed the names of certain bones (see the example for the bones of the wrist).

Factors in the evaluation of a patient—

SOAP

S — Subjective
O — Objective
A — Assessment
P — Plan

What a physician is supposed to pay attention to when admitting a patient to the hospital—

D. C. VAN DISSEL

D — Diagnosis
C — Condition
V — Vital signs

A — Ambulation
N — Nursing orders
D — Diet
I — Intake and output
S — Symptomatic drugs
S — Specific drugs
E — Examinations
L — Laboratory

Functions of blood—

Old **C**harlie **F**oster **H**ates **W**omen **H**aving **D**ull **C**lothes.

O — Oxygen (transport)
C — Carbon Dioxide (transport)
F — Food
H — Heat
W — Waste
H — Hormones
D — Disease
C — Clotting

For the properties of bile—

> Bile from the liver emulsifies greases
> Tinges the urine and colors the faeces
> Aids peristalsis, prevents putrefaction
> If you remember all this you'll give satisfaction.

Here's one that's almost too good to be true: a checklist of factors that could be causing back pain using the name of the Flemish anatomist who was among the first to describe the spine in detail—

O, VESALIUS

O — Osteomyelitis
V — Vertebral fracture
E — Extraspinal tumors
S — Spondylolisthesis
A — Ankylosing spondylitis
L — Lumbar disk disease
I — Intraspinal tumors
U — Unhappiness
S — Stress

The four major types of wounds—
CLIP

C — Crush
L — Laceration
I — Incision
P — Puncture

The five drugs that can be put in an endotracheal (ET) tube—
ALIEN

A — Atropine
L — Lidocaine
I — Isuprel
E — Epinephrine
N — Narcan

The twelve cranial nerves (in sequence)—

On Old Olympus' Towering Top,
A Fat Arsed German Vas Sipping Hops.

or

On Old Olympus' Towering Top,
A Finn And German Viewed Some Hawks.

O — Olfactory
O — Optic
O — Oculomotor
T — Trochlear
T — Trigeminal
A — Abducens
F — Facial
A — Auditory
G — Glossopharyngeal
V — Vagus
S — Spinal Accessory
H — Hypoglossal

and to remember which of the cranial nerves have motor fibers (M), sensory fibers (S), or both (B)—

1	2	3	4	5	6	7
Some	Say	Money	Matters	But	My	Brother

8	9	10	11	12
Says	Better	Business	Makes	Money.

Superficial branches of the facial nerve—
Ten Zebras Bit My Cheek.

T — Temporal
Z — Zygomatic
B — Buccal
M — Mandibular
C — Cervical

The five layers of the scalp—
SCALP

S — Skin
C — Connective tissue
A — Aponeurosis
L — Loose connective tissue
P — Periosteum

The excretory organs of the body (those that produce useless or harmful materials)—
SKILL

S — Skin
K — Kidneys
I — Intestines
L — Liver
L — Lungs

The order of nerves through the superior orbital tissue in the skull—
Lazy French Tarts Lie Naked In Anticipation.

L — Lacrimal
F — Frontal
T — Trochlear
L — Lateral
N — Nasociliary
I — Internal
A — Abducent

The carpal bones of the wrist (using the names current in the 1940s)—

Never Lower Tillie's Pants, Mama Might Come Home.

N — Navicular
L — Lunate
T — Triquetrum
P — Pisiform
M — Multangular, Greater
M — Multangular, Lesser
C — Capitate
H — Hamate

Some of the names had changed by the 1960s, so the device became—

Swiftly Lower Tillie's Pants, To Try Coitus Here.

S — Scaphoid
L — Lunate
T — Triquetrum
P — Pisiform
T — Trapezium
T — Trapezoid
C — Capitate
H — Hamate

The nerves which enter the hand, found on the anterior surface of the wrist—

RUM

R — Radial
U — Ulnar
M — Median

and the clinical manifestations of their injury, in the same order—

Women's Christian Temperance Union

W — Wrist drop
C — Claw hand
T — Tunnel syndrome

Position in the hip of blood vessels and nerves working from the outside inwards—

NAVY

N — Nerve
A — Artery
V — Vein
Y — represents the crotch

Tendons and neurovascular structures inside the ankle bone—
Tall Dark Virgins Almost Never Hesitate.

T — Tibialis Posterior tendon
D — Digitorum Longus tendon (flexor)
V — Vein—Tibialis
A — Artery—Tibialis Posterior
N — Nerve—Tibialis
H — Hallis Longus tendon (flexor)

Amino acids are the chief components of proteins and are synthesized by living cells or are obtained through food. The essential ones (in order)—
The Little Idiot Vocalist Let Me Play Trumpet Horn.

T — Threonine
L — Leucine
I — Isoleucine
V — Valine
L — Lysine
M — Methionine
P — Phenylalanine
T — Tryptophan
H — Histidine

or
These Ten Valuable Amino acids Have Long Preserved Life In Man.
or (from Janet Fein)
This Line Proved Highly Valuable In Memorizing Ten Little Acids.
or
PVT. TIM HALL

all of which include A for Arginine, one that's only required for infants.

The sections of the intestinal tract, in order—
   Dow **J**ones **I**ndustrial **A**verages **C**losing **S**tock **R**eport.

D — Duodenum
J — Jejunum
I — Ileum
A — Appendix
C — Colon
S — Sigmoid colon
R — Rectum

A medical rhyme—

When the face is red, raise the head.
When the face is pale, raise the tail.

An ancient method of treating hangovers—

Last evening you were drinking deep,
So now your head aches. Go to sleep;
Take some boiled cabbage when you wake;
And there's the end of your headache.

Alexis (circa 350 B.C.)

A diet recommended by some pediatricians for a sick child—
BRAT

B — Bananas
R — Rice
A — Applesauce
T — Toast

A Food Chemist's Bedtime Story—

Vitamin A
Keeps the cold germs away
And tends to make meek people nervy.

B's what you need
When you're going to seed
And C is specific in scurvy.

Vitamin D
Makes the bones in your knee
Tough and hard for the service on Sunday.

While E makes hens scratch
And increases the hatch
And brings in more profits on Monday.

Vitamin F
Never bothers the chef
For this vitamin never existed.

G puts the fight
In the old appetite
And you eat all the foods that are listed.

So now when you dine
Remember these lines;
If long on this globe you will tarry.

Just try to be good
And pick out more food
From the orchard, the garden, the dairy.

E. J. Bowen, Oxford, England

Vitamins (from a Cheerios box) —

The vitamin called A has important connections
It aids in our vision and helps stop infections.
To vitamin C this ditty now comes,
Important for healing and strong healthy gums,
Done with both of these?
Here come the B's:

B1 for the nerves.
B2 helps the cells energize.
Digesting the Protein's
B6's prize.

Tired?

If you iron tonic need,
Eat more spinach, beet, and swede;
If your nerves are all awry,
Lettuce and onions try.

The poet isn't recommending cannibalism; "swede" is another name for rutabaga.

A formula for long life—

DEVIL
William H. Baumer, La Jolla, Calif.
U.S. Army Major General, retired

D — Diet
E — Exercise
V — Vitamins and minerals
I — Involvement
L — Love

(Spelled backwards it's "lived.")

Psychology

Psychology is the scientific study of the behaviors and mental processes of organisms. The field of psychology has a large number of concepts to be mastered. Memory aids play two parts— they are an area that psychologists study as well as a technique for remembering important psychological concepts. Many of Freud's ideas have mnemonic devices that help the student to remember the essential points.

The five goals of psychology—

PACED

P — Prediction
A — Application
C — Control
E — Explanation
D — Description

Different types of psychological perspectives (areas of specialization)—

B.B.C. Produced Heidi.

B — Biological
B — Behavioral
C — Cognitive
P — Psychodynamic
H — Humanistic

Gestalt psychology is the study of perception and behavior from the perspective of an organism's response to configurational

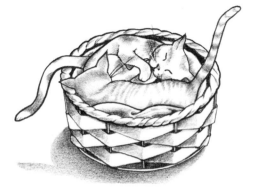

wholes with a stress on events. It rejects the idea of breaking the analysis down into separate elements. The Gestalt Grouping principles may be recalled with—

Cute Cozy Cats Sleep So Peacefully.

C — Closure
C — Common Fate
C — Continuity
S — Similarity
S — Simplicity
P — Proximity

Physical and Psychological dimensions of vision—
WACs love to watch CBS.

Physical	*Psychological*
W — Wavelength	C — Color
A — Amplitude	B — Brightness
C — Complexity	S — Saturation

Physical and Psychological dimensions of hearing—
WACs have Party Line Telephones

Physical	*Psychological*
W — Wavelength	P — Pitch
A — Amplitude	L — Loudness
C — Complexity	T — Timbre

The four major drug categories—
Drugs **S**ometimes **H**arm **M**e.

D — Depressants (slow the body functions)
S — Stimulants (speed up the body functions)
H — Hallucinogens (distort sensory perceptions)
M — Marijuana (intensifies sensory perceptions)

Hans Selye, a German physician, labeled the body's changes caused by stress as the General Adaptation Syndrome—
Some **GAS**es **ARE LETHAL**.

G — General
A — Adaptation
S — Syndrome

A — Alarm Stage
R — Resistance Stage
E — Exhaustion Stage

L — Lethargy
E — Elevated blood pressure, pulse
T — Tension
H — Headache
A — Anxiety
L — Low concentration

The words remembered with LETHAL are all symptoms of the syndrome.

Freud analyzed the human psyche and divided it into three parts. The id is that part which is associated with instinctual impulses and demands, thus the word itself is a mnemonic device for what it stands for. The ego is that part of the personality which is conscious and most immediately controls behavior. The superego is mainly unconscious and includes the perceived moral standards of the community. The three personality structures can be remembered with the word—
PIES

P — Personality =
I — Id +
E — Ego +
S — Superego

Freud stated that a child goes through various stages of psycho-sexual development as he matures. He identified five stages which can be recalled by using the sentence—

Oran **A**nd **P**hyllis **L**ike **G**iraffes.

O — Oral
A — Anal
P — Phallic
L — Latent
G — Genital

The phases of human sexual response according to the research team of Masters and Johnson—

EXPLORE

EX — Excitement
PL — Plateau
O — Orgasm
RE — Resolution

The three basic somatotypes (body types)—

ENDomorphs have big ends — They are soft and round.
Mesomorphs are **M**uscular — They are hard and muscular.
Ec**T**omorphs are **T**hin — They are skinny.

Pedomorph is a term used for an animal, such as a human, that requires an extended childhood.

The more common psychoanalytic techniques—

AFRAID

A   — Analysis of resistance
FR — Free association
A   — Analysis of transference
I   — Interpretation
D   — Dream analysis

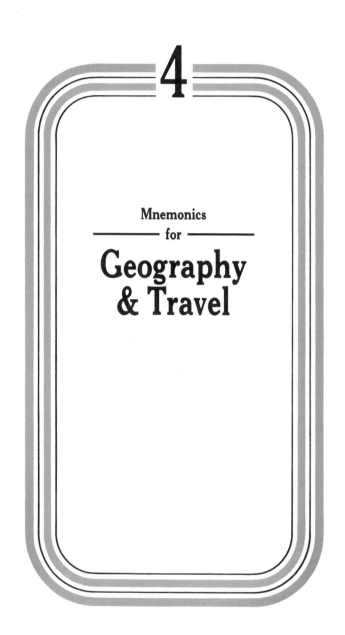

4

Mnemonics
— for —
**Geography
& Travel**

The study of geography and the lure of far-off places brings many strange words into our vocabularies. The term nautical mile or "nauts"—which is used at sea and in the air (1,852 meters or about 6,076 feet)—was originally measured on sailing ships by a "knotted" string tied to a log, timed with a 14-second hourglass.

Today's students are said to be very weak in locating countries or states on maps. Possibly the devices in this chapter will help.

A sentence to remember how to spell **GEOGRAPHY**—

George **E**liot's **O**ld **G**randmother
Rode **A** **P**ig **H**ome **Y**esterday.

or

George **E**ats **O**ld **G**ray **R**ats **A**t **P**aw's **H**ay **Y**ard.

In order to remember the two smallest countries in the world, use the phrase—

Very **M**inute

V — Vatican City — .16 sq. mi.
M — Monaco   — .4 sq. mi.

It is interesting to note that the smallest country in the world contains the largest church (St. Peter's—163,200 sq. ft.) and the

largest residence (Vatican Palace—1400 rooms and over 200 staircases). This means that Vatican City has the largest average household size of any country in the world. Legally Monaco may revert back to France if it does not have a male ruler, although Prince Rainier and Grace Kelly produced a male heir in 1958.

In the early years of the 20th century, the way a fashionable English ship traveler's luggage was marked indicated the location of his room(s) during the voyage, because it was the cooler, and therefore the more expensive, side of the ship on trips to India and back—

POSH—Port Out, Starboard Home

Maps/Globes

The points of the compass seem obvious once they have been learned, but young students use sentences to help them recall the four directions, in clockwise sequence—

Never Embrace Sexy Women.

N — North
E — East
S — South
W — West

And, slightly tamer versions—

Never Eat Soggy Waffles.
or
Never Eat Sour Watermelon.

Here are some geographic odds and ends—

Longitude — *long* lines — pole to pole

Latitude — like rungs of a *la*dder, or "Lats are flat" (horizontal)

Tropic of Cancer — "n" for north of the equator

Tropic of Capricorn — *lower* in the alphabet, *lower* on the globe

Number of Time Zones in the world — 24, the same as the number of hours in a day

Asia — the shortest name for the largest continent.

Australia — the smallest continent is also the only one with just one country.

The seven continents — Europe and the six A's
  Africa
  America, North
  America, South
  Antarctica
  Asia
  Australia

The five Olympic rings symbolize the five continents that participated in the revival of the Olympic games, omitting Antarctica (which I think should at least be included in the Winter Olympics) and Australia, which has since become extremely active in the Olympic movement.

Foreign Countries

The ten full members of the EEC (European Economic Community) may be recalled by visualizing a Guild Hall with ten hefty members—

BIG NF' GUILD

B — Belgium
I — Italy
G — Germany, West
N — Netherlands
F — France
G — Greece
U — United Kingdom
I — Ireland
L — Luxembourg
D — Denmark

The height of Mount Fujiyama—12,365 feet—can be remembered by thinking of a calendar (non-leap year variety)—

12 Months
365 Days

The Canadian provinces and territories, from west to east, from north to south—

You Need But Check A Short Mnemonic,
One Quickly Mastered Now.

Y — Yukon Territory
N — Northwest Territories
BC — British Columbia
A — Alberta
S — Saskatchewan
M — Manitoba
O — Ontario
Q — Quebec
M — Maritime provinces (New Brunswick, Nova Scotia,
      Prince Edward Island)
N — Newfoundland

Another sentence, from east to west, which breaks out the three
maritime provinces—

Nice **N**orthern **P**lace **N**estled **Q**uietly **O**ver
Many **S**tates **A**lways **B**efriending **N**eighboring **Y**ankees.

The countries across the top of Africa from west to east—
MALE around Tunisia—

M — Morocco
A — Algeria
L — Libya
E — Egypt

with little Tunisia squeezed in between Algeria and Libya.

How to remember where the Cape of Good Hope is (as opposed
to Cape Horn at the bottom of South America)—
ABC'FGH
Bill Sklar, New York, N.Y.

A — African
B — Bottom
C — Cape
'F — Of
G — Good
H — Hope

The countries of Africa that contain the letter Z are all in
southeast Africa and all touch one another—Zaire, Zambia,
Zimbabwe, Tanzania, and Mozambique—and this includes
the part of Africa where the Zulus are the dominant tribe.

The major islands off the west coast of Italy are in alphabetic order (from north to south) —

> Corsica (which belongs to France)
> Sardinia (Italian)
> Sicily (Italian)

You can remember that Corsica is French because it was Napoleon's birthplace (he was known as the "little Corsican").

The districts or states of Pakistan, from whence the name of the country was coined (in 1933) —

P   — Punjab
A   — Afghan
K   — Kashmir
S   — Sind
Tan — Baluchistan

The countries of Central America—both words contain seven letters, so there are seven countries and the area produces considerable fruit—

CHEaP aNd BiG

C — Costa Rica
H — Honduras
E — El Salvador
P — Panama
N — Nicaragua
B — Belize
G — Guatemala

A sentence to remember the above—

> **G**reat **B**ig **E**arthquakes **H**eave
> **N**ative **C**offee **P**lantations.

The three islands belonging to the Netherlands off the coast of Venezuela—

ABC

A — Aruba
B — Bonaire
C — Curacao

The two land-locked countries of South America can be recalled by realizing that, because they have no coastline, they are as dry as—

Parched Bones

Par — Paraguay
Bo — Bolivia

The nine largest islands in the world (in order) —
Green Guineas Born Mad Baffle Some Honest Great British Vicars.

Green	— Greenland	— 840,000 sq. mi.
Guinea	— New Guinea	— 306,000 sq. mi.
Born	— Borneo	— 280,100 sq. mi.
Mad	— Madagascar	— 226,658 sq. mi.
Baff	— Baffin	— 195,928 sq. mi.
Some	— Sumatra	— 165,000 sq. mi.
Hon	— Honshu	— 87,805 sq. mi.
Great British	— Great Britain	— 84,200 sq. mi.
Vic	— Victoria	— 83,896 sq. mi.

United States

The Great Lakes of the United States and Canada—
HOMES

H — Huron
O — Ontario
M — Michigan
E — Erie
S — Superior

You can recall the order of the lakes from east to west with—
Only **E**lephants **H**ave **M**assive **S**nouts.

Also, the largest (most superior) of these is Superior.

To remember the states that border the Great Lakes—
I'M NO WIMP
Mary Ann Cooper, Colorado Springs, Colo.

I   — Indiana
M — Michigan
N — New York
O — Ohio
W — Wisconsin
I   — Illinois
M — Minnesota
P — Pennsylvania

The eight major Hawaiian islands, from west to east—
No **K**id **O**f **M**ine **L**acks **M**y **K**inky **H**abits.
David Krieger, Springview, Neb.

N — Niihau
K — Kauai
O — Oahu
M — Molokai
L — Lanai
M — Maui
K — Kahoolawe
H — Hawaii

How to remember the relative size and age of the four large Hawaiian islands—

They are, in order from west to east:

Kauai (farthest west) is the smallest and the oldest.

Oahu (middle west) is the second smallest and second oldest.

Maui (middle east) is second largest and second youngest.

Hawaii (farthest east) is the largest (and still growing) and the youngest of all the islands.

The volcanic activity obviously is moving eastward.

How to remember which states touch the most other states—

Touches Most

T — Tennessee
Mo — Missouri

The four states that come together at one point, known as "Four Corners"—the only such point in the United States—

CANU

C — Colorado
A — Arizona
N — New Mexico
U — Utah

The peninsula that separates Chesapeake Bay from the Atlantic Ocean is refered to as the **Delmarva** peninsula, so named because it includes parts of the states of Delaware, Maryland, and Virginia.

How to remember what interstate highway numbers mean—

Odd numbers — North/South, starting at the west coast (old federal highways started at the east coast)

Even numbers — East/West, starting at the southern border (old federal highways started at the northern border)

Three digit numbers — first digit even — route through or around the city
— first digit odd   — spur into the city

What some Manhattanites call New Yorkers from the other four boroughs—

BBQ'S

B — Bronx
B — Brooklyn
Q — Queens
S — Staten Island

or
B & T's

B — Bridges
T — Tunnels

The only way to get to Manhattan Island is by a bridge or tunnel. You certainly wouldn't want to swim in the Hudson or East rivers.

Where the train stops on the main line out of Philadelphia—
Old Maids Never Wed And Have Babies.

O — Overbrook
M — Merion
N — Narberth
W — Wynnewood
A — Ardmore
H — Haverford
B — Bryn Mawr

Some U.S. cities have street names that were assigned in a particular pattern (other than just in numerical order). If you grow up in a city where the streets are named for U.S. Presidents in order by their terms of office, then that should help remembering the sequence of presidents at test time. In Albuquerque, New Mexico, the east-west streets in the downtown area are named for minerals in approximate order by their value, from south to north. In Austin, Texas, the streets around the capitol building are named for the major rivers of Texas, in order from west to east. Two of the more interesting cities with regard to their street names are:

Seattle, Washington — The east-west streets of the southern part of the downtown area share their first letter in pairs. The order of streets (from south to north) may be remembered by using—

Jesus Christ Made Seattle Under Protest.

J — Jefferson
J — James
C — Cherry
C — Columbia
M — Marion
M — Madison
S — Spring
S — Seneca
U — University

U — Union
P — Pike
P — Pine

Washington, D.C. — The major east-west streets were named
for important states in geographic order with Pennsylvania being
the keystone. Florida was originally Boundary street, because
there was no state of Florida. Potomac was originally Georgia,
which was moved elsewhere. The letter streets omit J because
they were based on the Roman alphabet. There are now four sets
of streets in alphabetic order, the second being two-syllable
words, the third being three-syllable words, and the fourth being
trees and plants.

Maritime

The four oceans of the world—
Pacific Is An Adjective.
Mike Leon, Fond du Lac, Wis.

P — Pacific ocean
I — Indian ocean
A — Atlantic ocean
A — Arctic ocean

The seven seas—
I see a sea map.

I — Indian ocean
C — Caribbean sea
A — Atlantic ocean
C — China sea
M — Mediterranean sea
A — Arctic ocean
P — Pacific ocean

There is no general agreement on what the "seven seas" are.
The dictionary defines the term as all the waters of the world.
Possibly the seven seas are the Mediterranean, Red, Black,
Baltic, North, Caspian, and China seas.

Left and Right on a naval vessel—Starboard has two R's, therefore it means right; Port has only one R so it means left. Also, the
words Port and Left both have four letters.

The running lights on naval vessels—
Red Port Wine

Red is on the port side, therefore green is on the starboard.

When facing seaward from inside a harbor, red buoys are on the left and black buoys are on the right. Therefore the way to know if a boat is coming back to port is—
Red Right Returning

and you can use the Elks Club insignia—
Brotherhood and Protective Order of Elks

to remember
Black Port On Entering.

A navigation ditty which tells the helmsman which side of a boat to pass—

Green to green or red to red,
Perfect safety, go ahead.
Red to green or green to red,
Drop the anchor, collision ahead.

How to remember the depth of a fathom—
Six letters, six feet

And a twain is two fathoms, which is the minimum navigable depth of the Mississippi. Samuel Clemens selected the pen name of Mark Twain from his days as a Mississippi river boat pilot.

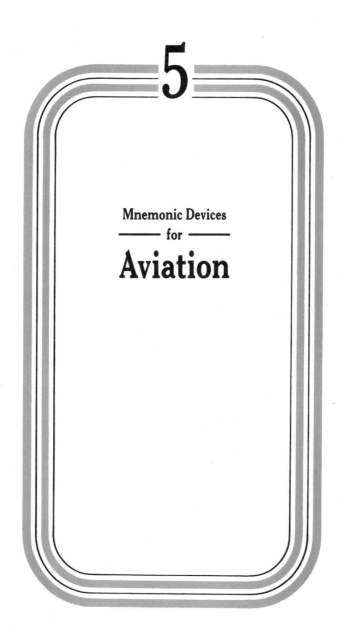

5

Mnemonic Devices
—— for ——
Aviation

Pilots have an interesting and often colorful selection of methods they use for various important things they need to remember. There is probably no greater testimonial to the value of mnemonic devices than the fact the pilots bet their lives on the accuracy of these memory aids. Crew members are also trained for various emergency situations with various acronyms.

At some airports there is a Visual Approach Slope Indicator system (VASI) that lets a pilot know whether or not he is approaching the airport landing strip at the proper angle. When approaching the runway at the correct slope, the downwind set of lights (those closest to the pilot) on both sides of the runway will appear white and the upwind lights (those farthest from the pilot) will appear red. The memory aid is—

> Red over red — you're going to be dead,
> White over white — you're high as a kite,
> Red over white — you're all right.

The following is a checklist for the documents required in the cockpit of an airplane—

ARROW

A — Airworthiness Certificate
R — Registration
R — Radio Permit
O — Owner's manual
W — Weight & Balance Control Form (describes the
        airplane's center of gravity)

There are many common sayings that are popular in the aviation business which reflect the common wisdom that comes from experience. Such as—

> There are old pilots,
> And bold pilots,
> But there are no old, bold pilots.

Federal Aviation Regulation 91.11 is very specific with regard to drinking and flying as a crew member of a civil aircraft—

> Eight hours from the bottle to the throttle

How to tell the direction the compass will swing when air speed changes—

ANDS

A — Accelerate N — North   D — Decelerate S — South

The magnetic north pole is not the same as the true north pole and therefore pilots must adjust for compass variation with respect to the line of zero magnetic variation. The adjustment is easily remembered with the rhyme—

> East is least (subtract)
> West is best (add)

This is also used for determining flying altitude—if you are flying east you fly at odd altitudes (e.g., 31,000 feet) since one, the first odd number, is less than two, the first even number. When flying west, you fly at even altitudes (e.g., 36,000 feet).

Here's a quick checklist to go over before you parachute out of your next flight in a fighter—

> Throttle,
> Bottle,
> Visor

In other words, decrease the speed by throttling back, take your oxygen bottle with you, and pull down the visor of your helmet in order to protect your eyes.

One of the best known aviation mnemonics is used to remember how to determine a compass heading—

True **V**irgins **M**ake **D**ull **C**ompany.

T — True Heading + /—
V — Variation =
M — Magnetic Heading + /—
D — Deviation =
C — Compass Heading

A variation of the sentence which was popular during World War II among flying cadets was "True virgins must dodge cadets."

Some pilots learn it in reverse order with the sentence—
Can Dead Men Vote Twice At Elections?

where the last two words mean to Add the variation for East (and therefore subtract for West).

Pilots use many different checklists for takeoffs, depending on the type of plane, who their instructor was, their interest in the opposite sex, etc. Some common ones—

CIGAR

C — Controls
I — Instruments
G — Gas
A — Attitude indicator
R — Radio

or
How To Make Pretty Females Sleep Close

H — Engine Hood, Hatches, Shoulder Harness
T — Cylinder and Oil Temperatures, Throttle Tension, Trim Tabs
M — Mixture, Magnetos
P — Pitot Head, Oil Pressure, Manifold Pressure, Pitch
F — Fuel, Flaps
S — Switches, Set Altimeter, Set Correct Time
C — Carburetor Heat, Canopy

When flying from a high-pressure area to a low-pressure area—

From high to low—
Watch out below.

This is because you are apt to experience unexpected dips in altitude as you enter a low-pressure area.

There are probably as many checklists for landings as there are for takeoffs. One of the better known—

GUMPS

G — Gas
U — Undercarriage (wheels)
M — Mixture
P — Pilot strapped in
S — Speed

There is a saying among pilots—"There are those that have, and those that shall . . ." (land with their wheels up).

All commercial airports have a three-letter code which is used on tickets, baggage claims, etc. Most of them are simply abbreviations of the city or metropolitan area name (e.g., DFW = Dallas-Fort Worth), but some are more difficult to remember. You can recall some of the more unusual ones with the following mnemonic devices—

FAT — Fresno, Calif. — the only **FAT** in Fresno
LAX — Los Angeles Intl. — L.A. is re**LAX**ed
MCO — Orlando, Fla. — **M**ickey's **CO**. (home of Disney World)
OGG — Maui, Hawaii — where men **OGG**le the girls
ORD — Chicago O'Hare — **O**rganized by Mayor **R**ichard **D**aley
SMF — Sacramento, Calif. — home of the **SM**ur**F**s
YUL — Montreal, Canada — **YUL**e-tide city

Private pilots are taught that if an emergency situation develops while in flight they should remember the four C's—

Confess — the predicament to any ground radio station without delay.

Communicate — with the ground radio link and pass on as much of the distress or alert message on the first transmission as possible.

Climb — in altitude, if possible, for better radar and direction-finding equipment detection.

Comply — with the advice and instructions received.

What a crew member asks or tells the Captain about, or concerning, a potential evacuation of a commercial flight—

TEST

T — Type of emergency (Equipment malfunction, Smoke in the cabin, Heart attack, etc.)
E — Evacuation (Is it required?)
S — Signal to be given by the Captain (Oral, Alarm, Lights, etc.)
T — Time (Number of minutes till evacuation)

Commercial aircraft crews are instructed that there are only certain situations when they can administer oxygen to a passenger. These can be remembered with—

IN USA

I — Irrational behavior
N — Note from passenger's doctor
U — Unconcious, but breathing
S — Severe chest pain
A — Asthma attack

Vietnam helicopter pilots were taught to consider these factors when selecting an airborne firing position—

BRASSCRAF

B — Background
R — Range
A — Altitude
S — Sun
S — Shadows
C — Cover & Concealment
R — Rotor wash
A — Avenues of approach and egress
F — Fields of fire

The direction of spin of helicopter rotor blades in the Free World (as seen by the pilot)—

Clockwise from the Cockpit.

In the Soviet bloc it's the reverse.

Here are the U.S. manned space mission programs, in chrono-logical order—

Many **G**entlemen **A**scend **S**kyward.
Kent O. McIntosh, Darmstadt, West Germany

M — Mercury
G — Gemini
A — Apollo
S — Skylab

How to remember the names of the twelve astronauts who have walked on the moon (each were members of two-man teams) —

AA — American astronauts (first landing)
CB — Radioing back information
SM — Space Missions
SI — Satellite Information
YD — Young Duke
CS — Curtain Show (last landing)

Commander shown first	*Date of lunar landing*	*Mission*
AA — Armstrong, Neil A.	7/20/1969	Apollo 11
Aldrin, Edwin E., Jr. ("Buzz")		
CB — Conrad, Charles, Jr.	11/18/1969	Apollo 12
Bean, Alan L.		

SM —	Shepard, Alan B., Jr. Mitchell, Edgar D.	2/03/1971	Apollo 14
SI —	Scott, David R. Irwin, James B.	7/30/1971	Apollo 15
YD —	Young, John W. Duke, Charles M., Jr.	4/20/1972	Apollo 16
CS —	Cernan, Eugene A. Schmidt, Harrison H.	12/11/1972	Apollo 17

The pattern of two landings a year was disrupted by the near disaster of Apollo 13 in April 1970 when the service module oxygen tank ruptured in flight; the crew of James Lovell, Jr., Fred Haise, Jr., and John Swigart, Jr., returned safely to earth by using the lunar module oxygen and power.

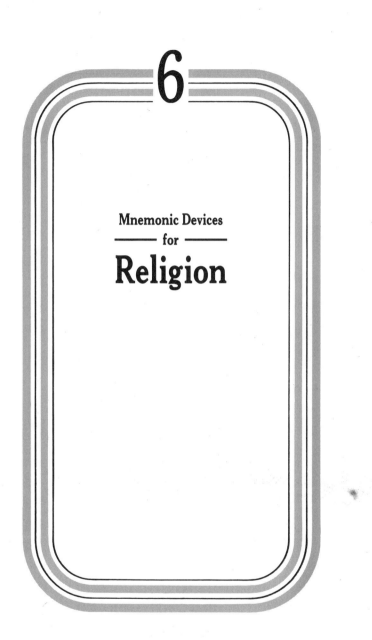

6

Mnemonic Devices
—— for ——
Religion

The major religions of the world are replete with examples of things that are memorized as an act of faith. Sunday school teachers have used mnemonic devices or brute force since time immemorial to "educate" their pupils. Herewith, a few:

Judaism/Old Testament

The Hebrews regard themselves as the chosen people—

> How odd
> Of God
> To choose
> The Jews.

The books of the Old Testament—

> The Great Jehovah speaks to us
> in Genesis and Exodus;
> Leviticus and Numbers see,
> Followed by Deuteronomy.
> Joshua and Judges sway the land
> Ruth gleans a sheaf with trembling hand.
> Samuel and numerous Kings appear,
> Whose Chronicles we wondering hear.
> Ezra and Nehemiah now,
> Esther, the beauteous mourner show,
> Job speaks in sighs, David in Psalms,
> The Proverbs teach to scatter alms.
> Ecclesiastes then come on,
> And the sweet Song of Solomon.
> Isaiah, Jeremiah then,
> With Lamentations takes his pen,
> Ezekiel, Daniel, Hosea's lyres,
> Swell Joel, Amos, Obadiah's.
> Next Jonah, Micah, Nahum come,
> And lofty Habakkuk finds room.
> While Zephaniah, Haggai calls,
> Rapt Zechariah builds his walls,
> And Malachi, with garments rent,
> CONCLUDES THE ANCIENT TESTAMENT.

You can remember God's covenant with Noah after the flood and his promise of what is to come with the couplet—

> God gave Noah the rainbow sign.
> No more water, the fire next time.

The plagues initiated by God to convince/punish Egypt in the time of Moses—

Retaliating **F**or **L**ong **F**rustration
Moses **B**adgered **H**ostile **L**eader **D**emanding **F**reedom.

R — River turned to blood
F — Frogs
L — Lice
F — Flies
M — Murrain (dire pestilence)
B — Boils
H — Hail
L — Locusts
D — Darkness
F — First-born killed

To remember the Ten Commandments, in order—
> **G**od **I**s **V**ery **S**ad;
> **H**e **K**illed **A** **S**mall **W**orld **C**oldly.
>> *Joseph O. Alford, Portage, Ind.*

G — No other Gods
I — no graven Images
V — no Vain use of the name
S — holy Sabbath
H — Honor parents
K — don't Kill
A — no Adultery
S — don't Steal
W — no false Witness
C — don't Covet

The location of the Ten Commandments in the Bible — Exodus 20

Remember the **X** (roman numeral ten) in Exodus and the **dus** on the end means two. Ten times two = 20.

Major figures in Judaism come in alphabetic as well as chronological order—

Abraham — founding patriarch, who is the father of
Isaac — who made a covenant with God, and was renamed
Israel — who is the father of
Jacob — who is the father of
Joseph.

The Minor Prophets (in order)—
> **H**ow **J**ust **A**nd **O**bedient **J**onah **M**ade **N**ineveh.

H — Hosea
J — Joel
A — Amos
O — Obadiah
J — Jonah
M — Micah
N — Nahum

Christianity/New Testament

Most Sunday school students have learned the names of the Four Gospels with—

> Matthew, Mark, Luke, and John
> Saddle my horse and I'll get on.

The New Testament (with abbreviations)—

> Matthew, Mark, Luke and John
> The Book of Acts then think upon,
> Romans, Cor., remember ye,
> Gal., Eph., Phi., Col., three T's, P.,
> Hebrews, James, Peter and John
> Jude and Revelation.

Christ's 12 disciples (sung to the tune of "Bringing in the Sheaves")—

> There were 12 disciples, Jesus called to help him.
> Simon Peter, Andrew, James, his brother John,
> Philip, Thomas, Matthew, James the son of Alphaeus,
> Thaddaeus, Simon, Judas, and Bartholemew.

The symbol for Christianity, used since the very early days of the church, is a fish. The Greek word for fish is **ICHTHYS,** which forms an acrostic of the Greek words for—

> Jesus Christ, Son Of God, Saviour.

This is one of the oldest mnemonic devices on record.

John Calvin, a French theologian (born Jean Chauvin) and religious reformer, was a leader in the Protestant movement in Switzerland and Scotland. The five tenets of Calvinism—

TULIP

T — Total depravity
U — Unconditional election
L — Limited atonement
I — Irresistible grace
P — Perseverance of the saints

Islam

The founder of Islam and the two holiest cities of the faith—

3 M's

Mohammed — the prophet was born in
Medina   — around 571 A.D. and later settled in
Mecca   — where the faithful are supposed to come on a
             pilgrimage at least once in their lifetime.

Hinduism

The four ways to God—

Jnanas Believe Knowledge Rates.

J — Jnana Yoga — The way to God through knowledge
B — Bhakti Yoga — The way to God through love
K — Karma Yoga— The way to God through work
R — Raja Yoga   — The way to God through psychological
                  exercise

Bhakti Yoga is the most widely practiced of the four.

Confucianism

Five terms that indicate goals of character and social life—

Gentle Confucius Loved The World.

Gen — Jen   — Ideal relationship between people
C   — Chun-tzu — True Manhood
L   — Li   — Propriety/Ritual of a well-conducted life
T   — Te   — Power/Arts of War
W   — Wen   — Culture/Arts of Peace

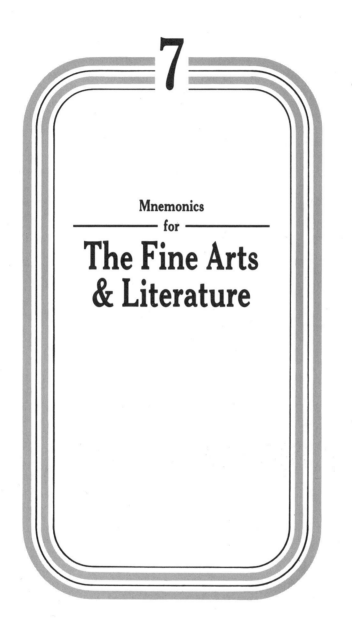

7

Mnemonics
—— for ——
The Fine Arts
& Literature

More people are exposed to mnemonics while studying music than any other field. Images and common words are particularly effective when teaching young children, who may not yet be able to understand the underlying concepts. Because memory aids are so widely used in this field, there are many variations of the same basic devices.

Music

Guido of Arezzo, in the 11th century, taught the musical notes of his day (Ut, Re, Mi, Fa, Sol, La) by using key syllables in his hymn to John the Baptist. Ut was later replaced by Do and Ti was added.

The notes, courtesy of *The Sound of Music*—

Do — a deer, a female deer
Re — a drop of golden sun
Mi — a name I call myself
Fa — a long, long way to run
So — a needle pulling thread
La — a note to follow So
Ti — a drink with jam and bread

that will bring us back to Do.

Major Composers of the Classical period (1750 A.D.–1815 A.D.)
Glorious Bells Have Many Beautiful Sounds.

G	—	Gluck	1714–1787
B	—	Bach, C.P.E.	1714–1788
H	—	Haydn	1732–1809
M	—	Mozart, W.A.	1756–1791
B	—	Beethoven	1770–1827
S	—	Schubert	1797–1828

Major Composers of the Romantic period (1815 A.D.–1900 A.D.)
**Summer Breezes Make Certain Sounds Like Wailing;
Very Basic Melodies To Murmur Delicious Secrets.**

S	—	Schubert	1797–1828
B	—	Berlioz	1803–1869
M	—	Mendelssohn	1809–1847
C	—	Chopin	1810–1849

S	—	Schumann	1810–1856
L	—	Liszt	1811–1886
W	—	Wagner	1813–1883
V	—	Verdi	1813–1901
B	—	Brahms	1833–1897
M	—	Mussorgsky	1839–1881
T	—	Tchaikovsky	1840–1893
M	—	Mahler	1860–1911
D	—	Debussy	1862–1918
S	—	Strauss, Richard	1864–1949

Major Composers of the 20th century—

Sometimes **I**n **R**eading **B**ooks **S**o **W**rongly **B**ent, **P**rotagonists **H**ave **C**uriously **C**aused **C**rimes **P**urely **D**eviant.

S	—	Schoenburg	1874–1951
I	—	Ives	1874–1954
R	—	Ravel	1875–1937
B	—	Bartok	1881–1945
S	—	Stravinsky	1882–1971
W	—	Webern	1883–1945
B	—	Berg	1885–1935
P	—	Prokofiev	1891–1953
H	—	Hindemith	1895–1963
C	—	Copland	1900–
C	—	Carter	1908–
C	—	Cage	1912–
P	—	Penderecki	1933–
D	—	Davidovsky	1934–

All-time greats of German Music—

The three **B**'s

Bach
Beethoven
Brahms

Classification of musical voices—

STAB

S	—	Soprano
T	—	Tenor
A	—	Alto
B	—	Bass

The placement of notes in musical notation:

The notes on the lines of the Treble Clef (from the bottom up) —

Every **G**ood **B**oy **D**oes **F**ine.

Some music teachers use "**E**very **G**ood **B**ird **D**oes **F**ly" for the treble clef, since birds would fly in the highest lines. In England the words "deserves favour" are substituted for "does fine." Other words used with "deserves" are "fruit" and "fudge."

The notes in the spaces between the lines of the Treble Clef (from the bottom up) —

FACE

Bass Clef — Lines

Good **B**oys **D**eserve **F**udge **A**lways.

Bass Clef — Spaces

All **C**ows **E**at **G**rass

or

All **C**ars **E**at **G**as

Names of the sharps (in order)—

Father **C**alls **G**race **D**arling **A**fter **E**ating **B**uns.

or

Frederick **C**hopin **G**oes **D**own **A**nd **E**nds **B**attle.

F — 1st sharp
C — 2nd sharp
G — 3rd sharp
D — 4th sharp
A — 5th sharp
E — 6th sharp
B — 7th sharp

Note: The flats are the same but in reverse order.

The names of the six guitar strings from lowest to highest—

Even **A**fter **D**inner **G**iraffes **B**end **E**asily.

Nancy Rempe, Dallas, Texas

The four sections of a Symphony Orchestra—

Sinners **W**ill **B**e **P**unished.

S — String section
W — Woodwind section
B — Brass section
P — Percussion section

Instruments in a Symphony Orchestra—

String section—

Viper's **V**ile **V**enom **D**iscontinues **B**reathing.

V — Violin
V — Viola
V — Violoncello
D B — Double Bass

Woodwind section—

Peter's **F**riend **C**lara **B**rought
Elegant **B**oxes **O**f **C**hocolate.

P — Piccolo
F — Flute
C — Clarinet
B — Bass Clarinet
E — English Horn
B — Bassoon

O — Oboe
C — Contra Bassoon

The English Horn is misleading as it is not a horn but a double-reeded instrument.

Brass section—

Sharon **C**alled **T**o **F**ind
Her **T**iny **T**errier—**B**runo.

S   — Saxophone
C   — Cornet
T   — Trumpet
F H — French Horn
T   — Trombone
T   — Tuba
B   — Bass Tuba

Percussion section—

Tom's **X**-ray **S**howed **B**roken **B**ones,
Torn **C**artilage, **T**angled **T**endons,
Crushed **G**izzards, **C**reating **G**reat **P**ain.

T — Timpani
X — Xylophone
S — Snare Drum
B — Bass Drum
B — Bells
T — Tom-Tom
C — Castanets
T — Triangle
T — Tambourine
C — Cymbals
G — Gong
C — Chime
G — Glockenspiel
P — Piano

Literature

How to remember what not to do with borrowed books (from a bookplate)—

Who folds a leaf down,
The devil toast brown.
Who makes mark or blot,

The devil roast hot.
Who steals this book,
The devil shall cook.

The Shakespearean comedies, in the order of their composition—

**Errol loves two tame midtown merchants;
much merriment. Alas, 'twill always
mean triangles.**

Errol   — Comedy of Errors
loves   — Love's Labour's Lost
two   — Two Gentlemen of Verona
tame   — Taming of the Shrew
midtown   — Midsummer Night's Dream
merchants   — Merchant of Venice
much   — Much Ado About Nothing
merriment   — Merry Wives of Windsor
Alas   — As You Like It
twill   — Twelfth Night
always   — All's Well That Ends Well
mean   — Measure for Measure
triangles   — Troilus and Cressida

Mythology

The male symbol and the female symbol may be remembered
easily if you know what they stand for—

Male symbol   — Shield and sword of Mars

Female symbol   — Hand mirror of Venus

The nine Muses, all daughters of Zeus and Mnemosyne (see
Dedication), divide rather easily into two groups—the Muses of
Poetry and all the others. The four Muses of Poetry can be re-
called by visualizing a dripping "L"—

Ells Ceep

E — Epic   C — Calliope
L — Love   E — Erato
L — Lyric   E — Euterpe
S — Sacred   P — Polyhymnia

Note that each list is in alphabetic order. The remaining five are a little harder—

All **C**ould **D**o **H**ard **T**hings.
Yo**U** **T**ry **T**o **C**lue **M**e.

A — Astronomy	U — Urania (remember the planet)
C — Comedy	T — Thalia (contains an H for Humor)
D — Dance	T — Terpsichore (trips while dancing)
H — History	C — Clio (I and O in History)
T — Tragedy	M — Melpomene (M and O in Moody)

The seven dwarves of Snow White fame (in alphabetic order)—

Beautiful **D**reamy **D**amsel
Grooms **H**airy **S**hort **S**idekicks.

B — Bashful
D — Doc
D — Dopey
G — Grumpy
H — Happy
S — Sleepy
S — Sneezy

Show Business

The three note musical logo of the National Broadcasting Company is G, E, C, because it was originally owned by the General Electric Corporation (and has been re-purchased by GE). That's what those three notes between programs are!

You can remember the movies featuring the Marx Brothers, 13 in all, with several different tricks. Movies 2–5 all have animals in the title, the middle five spell **DORRC**, there are 2 nights and 2 days. They may be remembered, in sequence, with the sentence—

Could **A**ny **M**ovie **H**ouse **D**eny **O**ne **R**eally **R**are **C**lip
With **S**tar **C**omedians **L**aughing?

Cocoanuts (1929)
Animal Crackers (1930)
Monkey Business (1931)
Horse Feathers (1932)
Duck Soup (1933)

A Night at the Opera (1935)
A Day at the Races (1936)
Room Service (1938)
A Day at the Circus (1938)
Go West (1940)
The Big Store (1941)
A Night in Casablanca (1946)
Love Happy (1950)

Many of Paul Newman's mid-career movies may be remembered with the letter "**H**"

The Helen Morgan Story	— 1957
The Long Hot Summer	— 1958
The Left Handed Gun	— 1958
Cat on a Hot Tin Roof	— 1958
Hustler	— 1961
Hud	— 1963
Harper	— 1966
Hombre	— 1967
Cool Hand Luke	— 1967
The Secret War of Harry Frigg	— 1967

The first five James Bond movies, all starring Sean Connery, were in alphabetic order—

Dr. No	(1962)
From Russia With Love	(1963)
Goldfinger	(1964)
Thunderball	(1965)
You Only Live Twice	(1967)

Sean came back to do *Diamonds Are Forever* (1971) and *Never Say Never Again* (1985). Roger Moore did seven Bond movies from 1973 to 1985. Apparently, no one cares enough about them to create a mnemonic.

8

Mnemonic Devices
——— for ———
The Language Arts

You probably use several mnemonic devices for remembering how to spell or pronounce difficult words. This area abounds with rhymes and simple catch phrases that young children use to come to grips with how to use a language. Mnemonics play an important part in the education of the learning disabled, especially those with Attention Deficit Disorder. The Shelton School in Dallas has been kind enough to share their techniques and training aids with me. They also held a contest among their students to encourage them to create their own devices, some of which I have included here.

Basic Education—

The three **R**'s — **R**eading, '**R**iting, and '**R**ithmetic

Spelling

When children first begin looking up words in the dictionary it is handy to know what quartile (¼th of the book) a word will be found in. This can be remembered with the phrase—

Angry **E**lephants **M**adly **S**quirt.

or

Angry **E**lephants **M**ash **S**piders.

A to E — First 25% of the words in the dictionary
E to M — Second 25% of the words in the dictionary

M to S — Third 25% of the words in the dictionary
S to Z — Fourth 25% of the words in the dictionary

Spelling and Pronunciation Rules

One reason that we need memory tricks to remember how to spell is that there are so many exceptions to the rules. There are some rules, however, which help.

Probably the most commonly memorized rule for spelling (which is fraught with exceptions) —

> **I before E
> except after C
> or when sounded like A
> as in neighbor or weigh.**

Exceptions—

> Neither leisured foreign counterfeiter could seize
> either weird height without forfeiting protein.

> Einstein studied ancient science.

By remembering the exceptions you will also remember how to spell those words correctly.

There are several other sentences like those exceptions above that are collections of words with similar spelling problems. Some of them are:

"ei" words — Our neighbor's eight beige reindeer weighed too much to send by freight.

"silent g" words — The gnarled gnome gnashed his teeth as he gnawed a gnat.

"silent h" words — A rheumatic rhinoceros practices rhetorical rhymes while eating rhododendrons and rhubarb in Rhode Island.

"plural" words — There were heroes facing torpedoes while eating tomatoes and potatoes.

"tough" words — I thought I'd bought enough cough syrup to make it through this rough, tough winter.

Words that end in -*ful* and mean "full of" always have one "l." There are no exceptions. Isn't that wonderful?

When a word ends in "y", change the "y" to "i" before adding the suffixes *-ly, -ness,* or *-age.*

busy   — business
day   — daily
lonely — loneliness
marry — marriage

There are only a few exceptions, such as:

shy   — shyly
sly   — slyly

Remember to keep the "y" when adding *-ing.*

The "floss" rule—

one-syllable words that end in F, L, or S after a short vowel will most often use two of the letter

as in   SNIFF, HILL, PASS

A rule for suffixes—

The E will fly
Before you try
To add a vowel ending.

For example, come + ing = coming
bake + ed = baked

Spelling Tricks

A technique for remembering how to spell tricky words is to emphasize the syllable in question vocally or in your mind as you are spelling it. This may even include mispronouncing the word in order to remember the correct spelling. Some examples:

an es THET ic
co OP er ate
feb RU ary
la BOR a tory
li BRAR y
med I EV AL

The following list, in alphabetic order, is a collection of many different types of tricks for remembering how to spell words correctly. Mnemonic devices for spelling are used more frequently than any other type of memory aid.

ache	— I have *a chest* ache.
allegiance	— *All* pledge allegiance to the *giant.*
altar	— An al*tar* is a *table.*
alter	— You al*ter* the *terms* of a contract.
amendment	— An a*mend*ment *mends* the law.
architect	— The *arch* was designed by an *archi*tect.
arithmetic	— To spell it, remember this sentence:

A Rat In The House May Eat The Ice Cream

assassin	— The *assass*in was a double *ass.*
assume	— Assume can make an "ass" of "u" and "me."
bachelor	— *Bach* was not a bachelor.
believe	— Believe has a "lie" in it.
borough	— You can remember how to spell borough because it's "rough" in there.
cemetery	— You get your "ease" in the cemetery. (Three e's—No a's.)
committee	— MM, TT, and EE met in a committee.
Connecticut	— *Connecti*cut *connects* New York to Rhode Island.
conscience	— Does *science* have a con*science?*
desert	— Desert has one "s" because it is **s**o dry.
dessert	— Dessert has two "s"'s because it is **s**o **s**weet.
ecstasy	— There's no "x" in ecstasy.
embarrass	— Use this sentence:

Every Mother Beams At Reared Rascals Achieving Scholarly Success.

friend	— A friend is a fri*end* to the *end.*
knowledge	— You get an *edge* with knowl*edge.*
mnemonics	— A sentence to remember how to spell it:

Mnemonics Neatly Eliminate Man's Only Nemesis; Insufficient Cerebral Storage.

William D. Harvey

monotonous	— Four "o"'s in a word get monotonous.
nausea	— Remember that nausea has a "sea" in it.
separate	— To spell "separate" remember that it contains "a rat."
skiing	— You should use both "eyes" when skiing.
Tennessee	— NN, SS, and EE met in Tennessee.
together	— We go together "to get her."
twelfth	— There's an elf in twelfth.
weather	— The weather lady had to *eat her* words.

Grammar

The nine parts of speech—

1. Three little words you often see,
   are articles—a, an, and the.
2. A noun's the name of any thing,
   as school or garden, hoop or swing.
3. Adjectives tell the kind of noun,
   as great, small, pretty, white or brown.
4. Instead of nouns the pronouns stand,
   her head, his face, your arm, my hand.
5. Verbs tell of something to be done,
   to read, count, sing, laugh, jump and run.
6. How things are done the adverbs tell,
   as slowly, quickly, ill or well.
7. Conjunctions join the words together,
   as men and women, wind or weather.
8. The preposition stands before
   a noun as at or through the door.
9. The interjections show surprise,
   as ah! how pretty, oh! so wise.

> The whole are called the parts of speech,
> which reading, writing, speaking teach.

A method of remembering when to use capitalization—

Dinner MINTS

D — Days of the week
M — Months of the year
I — I, when it is used as a word
N — Names of people, places, and things
T — Titles of books, plays, royalty, etc.
S — Start of a sentence

Also, you can remember what words not to use at the start of a sentence by using the phrase—

A Terrible Boo Boo

A — And
T — Then
B — But
B — Because

A technique for teaching children the use of prepositions is to draw a cloud and an airplane on separate pieces of paper. The airplane can then be moved UNDER the cloud, OVER the cloud, BEHIND the cloud, etc. to demonstrate that prepositions show relationships.

Good writing, especially journalism, seeks to answer six basic questions. Kipling paid homage to his six serving men in this poem—

> I keep six honest serving men
> (They taught me all I knew):
> Their names are What and Why and When
> And How and Where and Who.
>
> *Rudyard Kipling*

Pronunciation

How to pronounce * (asterisk)—

> Mary had an aero-plane,
> About the clouds to frisk.
> Now wasn't she a silly thing,
> Her little *

Mnemosyne (the Goddess of Memory—see the dedication of this book) had two "knees." (knee maas n knee)

There is no "cow" in Moscow. (It is a long "o.")

Definitions

Horizontal — Flat like the horizon, therefore vertical is up and down.

Metaphor — stronger than a simile in that it assigns one object's characteristics to another (e.g., "He is an old bear.")

Simile — shares three letters with the word "like"—uses the word "like" or "as" in comparing two objects (e.g., "He's as grouchy as an old bear in the morning").

Foreign Languages

The most obvious mnemonic device for foreign languages is when the word is very similar in both languages (e.g., "Brot" in German is "bread" in English, "Huhn" is "hen"). But there are others that may prove helpful to students of a foreign tongue.

French

French verbs conjugated with the helping verb "être"—
MRS. R.D. VANDERTRAMP

M — Monter	—	Go up
R — Rester	—	Stay
S — Sortir	—	Go out
R — Retourner	—	Return
D — Devenir	—	Became
V — Venir	—	To come
A — Aller	—	Go
N — Naître	—	Be born
D — Descendre	—	Go down
E — Entrer	—	Enter
R — Rentrer	—	Return
T — Tomber	—	Fall
R — Revenir	—	Come back
A — Arriver	—	Arrive, Happen
M — Mourir	—	To die
P — Partir	—	Leave

German

German pronunciation of the combination IE—

> When I and E go walking,
> The E does the talking.

In German IE is pronounced "E" while EI is pronounced "I."

Definite Articles—

	Masculine	Feminine	Neuter	Plural
Nominative	der	die	das	die
Genitive	des	der	des	der
Dative	dem	der	dem	den
Accusative	den	die	das	die

Sung to the tune of "Turkey in the Straw"—

> Oh the masculine changes from der to den,
> And the feminine, neuter, and plural stay the same.
> In the dative case it's really a shame,
> Its dem, der, dem, and the plural is den.

> Look at the genitive, see what it does.
> Look at the genitive, see what it has.
> It's des, der, des, der—
> > whoever has something hasn't a care.

Prepositions that govern the dative case—

> > Roses are red,
> > Violets are blue,
> > Aus, bei, mit, nach, seit, von, zu.
> > > *Dr. Laurence F. McNamee, Commerce, Texas*

Hebrew

Pronunciation of Hebrew pronouns and their English translation—

Hebrew pronunciation		*English translation*
Me	=	Who
Who	=	He
He	=	She

Latin

For the common verbs that govern the dative case—

> > A Dative put, remember, pray,
> > After envy, spare, obey
> > Persuade, believe, command—to these
> > Add pardon, succor and displease.
> > With vacare, to have leisure
> > Add placere, to give pleasure.
> > With nubere, of the female said:
> > The English of it is 'to wed'.
> > Servire add and add studere
> > Favor, resist and indulgere.

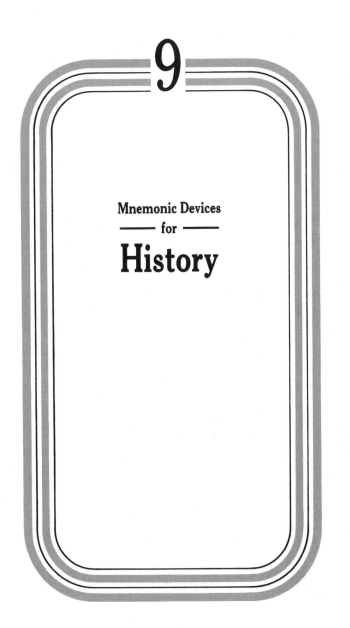

9

Mnemonic Devices
—— for ——
History

It has become a cliché to say that it isn't important to know exactly when something happened as long as you know the relative sequence of events. You will find mnemonics in this chapter to help you remember both specific dates and sequences. There are ways of remembering Roman Emperors, Kings and Queens of England, and American Presidents. The devices are arranged in chronological sequence by section.

World History

You can remember the ancient Greek Tribes with the word—
AID

A — Aeolic
I — Ionic
D — Doric

The Four Horsemen of the Apocalypse as described in the Book of Revelation—
Please Don't Waste Food.

P — Pestilence
D — Death
W — War
F — Famine

Rome is located on seven hills which can be recalled with the
sentence—

Could Queen Victoria Eat Cold Apple Pie?

C — Capitoline
Q — Quirinal
V — Viminal
E — Esquiline
C — Caelian
A — Aretine
P — Palatine

Julius Caesar was recognized as a military genius. A device to
remember the most important battles of his career is—

Is Perpetual Zeal The Means?

I — Ilerda
P — Pharsalus
Z — Zeta
T — Thapsus
M — Munda

After Julius Caesar was assassinated in 44 B.C. there were thir-
teen years of civil war. Caesar's heir and adopted son Octavian
led a faction to victory and was given the title of Augustus. He
founded the Roman Empire in 27 B.C. and it lasted until 395 A.D.
when it was divided with Constantinople as the eastern capital.
The early Roman Emperors (in sequence)—

At The Canine Club Never Give Out
Viscous Vegetables To Dalmatians.

A — Augustus	27 B.C.–A.D. 14
T — Tiberius	A.D. 14–37
C — Caligula	37–41
C — Claudius	41–54
N — Nero	54–68
G — Galba	68–69
O — Otho	69
V — Vitellius	69
V — Vespasian	69–79
T — Titus	79–81
D — Domitian	81–96

The Kings and Queens of England—

> Willy, Willy, Harry, Ste,
> Harry, Dick, John, Harry three,
> One, Two, Three Neds, Richard two,
> Henry Four, Five, Six—then who?
> Edward Four, Five, Dick the Bad,
> Harries twain and Ned the Lad,
> Mary, Bessie, James the Vain,
> Charlie, Charlie, James again.
> William and Mary, Anna Gloria,
> Four Georges, William and Victoria.
> Ned Seventh ruled till 1910,
> When George the Fifth came in, and then
> Ned went when Mrs. Simpson beckoned,
> Leaving George and Liz the Second.

Anonymous

Willy	— William I	— 1066–1087
Willy	— William II	— 1087–1100
Harry	— Henry I	— 1100–1135
Ste	— Stephen	— 1135–1154
Harry	— Henry II	— 1154–1189
Dick	— Richard I	— 1189–1199
John	— John	— 1199–1216
Harry Three	— Henry III	— 1216–1272
Ned One	— Edward I	— 1272–1307
Ned Two	— Edward II	— 1307–1327
Ned Three	— Edward III	— 1327–1377
Richard Two	— Richard II	— 1377–1400
Henry Four	— Henry IV	— 1399–1413
Henry Five	— Henry V	— 1413–1422
Henry Six	— Henry VI	— 1422–1471
Edward Four	— Edward IV	— 1461–1483
Edward Five	— Edward V	— 1483–1483
Dick the Bad	— Richard III	— 1483–1485
Harry	— Henry VII	— 1485–1509
Harry	— Henry VIII	— 1509–1547
Ned the Lad	— Edward VI	— 1547–1553
Mary	— Mary I	— 1553–1558
Bessie	— Elizabeth I	— 1558–1603
James the Vain	— James I	— 1603–1625
Charlie	— Charles I	— 1625–1649
		1653–1658 Oliver Cromwell

				1658–1659	Richard Cromwell
Charlie	—	Charles II	—	1660–1685	
James again	—	James II	—	1685–1701	
William and	—	William III	—	1689–1702	
Mary	—	Mary II	—	1694	
Anna Gloria	—	Anne	—	1702–1714	
George	—	George I	—	1714–1727	
George	—	George II	—	1727–1760	
George	—	George III	—	1760–1820	
George	—	George IV	—	1820–1830	
William	—	William IV	—	1830–1837	
Victoria	—	Victoria	—	1837–1901	
Ned Seventh	—	Edward VII	—	1901–1910	
George the Fifth	—	George V	—	1910–1936	
Ned	—	Edward VIII	—	1936–1936	
George	—	George VI	—	1936–1952	
Liz the Second	—	Elizabeth II	—	1952–	

Alternative:

> Working wives seldom had really jazzy hemlines.
> Triple-E rubbers hardly help.
> Hairstyles everywhere even resemble haystacks,
>   higher every month, enormous!
> Jolly courtiers clothe jades, whose men are grateful
>   for what virility endures;
> Gaudy, effete gentlemen expire, cheering.

The phrase "grateful for" stands for the first four Georges. The mnemonic errs in not mentioning William III as reigning apart from Mary. The last word anticipates Charles III.

The English Royal Houses—
     No Plan Like Yours To Study History Wisely.

N	—	Norman	—	1066–1135
P	—	Plantaganet	—	1154–1400
L	—	Lancaster	—	1399–1471
Y	—	York	—	1461–1485
T	—	Tudor	—	1485–1603
S	—	Stuart	—	1603–1714
H	—	Hanover	—	1714–1901
W	—	Windsor	—	1901–

The name "House of Windsor" was adopted 7/17/1917 during the First World War. Previously it was known as the House of Saxe-Coburg and Gotha, but German names became rather unpopular in England during this period of time.

The disposition of Henry VIII's six wives (in order) —

Divorced, beheaded, died,
Divorced, beheaded, survived

(Catherine of Aragon, Ann Boleyn, Jane Seymour,
Anne of Cleves, Catherine Howard, and Catherine Parr)

or

Bluff Henry the Eighth to six spouses was wedded:
One died, one survived, two divorced, two beheaded.

The battles in the War of the Roses, 1455–1485 (so called because of the white rose emblem of the House of York and the red rose emblem of the House of Lancaster) —

A Boy **N**ow **W**ill **M**ention
All **T**he **H**ot **H**orrid **B**attles **T**ill **B**osworth.

A — St. Albans
B — Blore Heath
N — Northhampton
W — Wakefield
M — Mortimer's Cross
A — St. Albans (2nd)
T — Towton
H — Hedgeley Moor
H — Hexham
B — Bornet
T — Tewkesbury
B — Bosworth

The following are couplets that help you recall the year that an historical event occurred.

William the Conqueror, Ten Sixty-Six
Played on the Saxons oft-cruel tricks.

In Fourteen Hundred and Ninety-Two,
Columbus sailed the ocean blue.

The Spanish Armada met its fate,
in Fifteen Hundred and Eighty-Eight.

In Sixteen Hundred and Sixty-Six
London burnt like rotten sticks.

George the Third said with a smile,
Seventeen Sixty yards in a mile.

(This conveys two facts—the year of his ascension to the English throne and the number of yards in a mile.)

The way to remember Joseph Stalin's birthdate and location—

His gory life started on the darkest day.

Stalin was born December 21, 1879, in the Transcaucasian town of Gori, Soviet Georgia. Stalin's date of death is also unusual—

3/5/53

American History

A poem to remember when the Revolutionary War began—

'Twas the eighteenth of April in '75,
Hardly a man is now alive,
That remembers that famous day and year
Of the midnight ride of Paul Revere. . . .
Henry Wadsworth Longfellow

The presidents of the United States (in order of their administrations)—

Washington And **Jefferson** **M**ade **M**any **A** **J**oke.
Van Buren **H**ad **T**roubles **P**lenty **T**o **F**ind.
Pierce **B**oasted **L**oud; **Johnson** **G**ave **H**im **G**ood **A**dvice.
Cleveland **H**ailed **Cleveland**, **M**ade **R**uler **T**wice.
Wilson **H**ad **C**ourage **H**owever **R**epublicans
Turned **E**lsewhere.
Kennedy **J**oked **N**ot **F**or **C**lear **R**easons.

W — Washington   — 1789–1797
A — Adams (John)   — 1797–1801
J — Jefferson   — 1801–1809
M — Madison   — 1809–1817
M — Monroe   — 1817–1825
A — Adams (John Quincy)   — 1825–1829
J — Jackson   — 1829–1837
V — Van Buren   — 1837–1841
H — Harrison (William Henry)   — 1841–1841
T — Tyler   — 1841–1845

P	— Polk	—	1845–1849
T	— Taylor	—	1849–1850
F	— Fillmore	—	1850–1853
P	— Pierce	—	1853–1857
B	— Buchanan	—	1857–1861
L	— Lincoln	—	1861–1865
J	— Johnson (Andrew)	—	1865–1869
G	— Grant	—	1869–1877
H	— Hayes	—	1877–1881
G	— Garfield	—	1881–1881
A	— Arthur	—	1881–1885
C	— Cleveland	—	1885–1889
H	— Harrison (Benjamin)	—	1889–1893
C	— Cleveland	—	1893–1897
M	— McKinley	—	1897–1901
R	— Roosevelt (Teddy)	—	1901–1909
T	— Taft	—	1909–1913
W	— Wilson	—	1913–1921
H	— Harding	—	1921–1923
C	— Coolidge	—	1923–1929
H	— Hoover	—	1929–1933
R	— Roosevelt (Franklin)	—	1933–1945
T	— Truman	—	1945–1953
E	— Eisenhower	—	1953–1961
K	— Kennedy	—	1961–1963
J	— Johnson (Lyndon)	—	1963–1969
N	— Nixon	—	1969–1974
F	— Ford	—	1974–1977
C	— Carter	—	1977–1981
R	— Reagan	—	1981–1989

A clever poem that runs from Washington to Carter—

> Wilma's apple jelly makes men adore jam.
> Vera's hot tamales peel the frying pan.
> Bertha's lasagne just gives her gas.
> And Carmen's homemade chili makes
> Roy's teacher whip his class.
> Help Roy's teacher.
> Eleven kooks justify nailing four cooks.
>   *Joan Campbell, Los Osos, Calif.*

There is an interesting mnemonic device for remembering all
the presidents who were assassinated plus all but one who died

in office. It is called **The Rule of 20s**. Every president elected in a year divisible by 20 since 1840 has died in office—Reagan being the exception. Zachary Taylor died in office on July 9th, 1850—the only death in office not included below.

1840 — William Henry Harrison — died of pneumonia after 30 days in office (April 4, 1841)

1860 — Abraham Lincoln — shot by John Wilkes Booth and died April 15, 1865 (in his second term)

1880 — James Abram Garfield — shot by Charles J. Guiteau and died September 19, 1881

1900 — William McKinley — shot by Leon Czolgosz and died September 14, 1901

1920 — Warren Gamaliel Harding — died August 2, 1923, in San Francisco, California

1940 — Franklin Delano Roosevelt — died April 12, 1945 (in his fourth term)

1960 — John Fitzgerald Kennedy — shot by Lee Harvey Oswald and died November 22, 1963

The religion and ethnic background of the presidents is easily remembered because all have been male **WASP**s (**W**hite **An**glo **S**axon **P**rotestants) with the exception of Kennedy, whose religion was Catholicism.

The Bill of Rights—
REQUISITES for freedom.
Howard F. Harrell, Rockville, Md.

R — Religious and other freedoms (**ASP** Assembly, Speech, Press)

E — Establishment of militia and right to bear arms

Q — Quartering of troops proscribed

U — Unreasonable search and seizure protected against

I — Incrimination of self not compelled

S — Speedy public impartial trial by due process

I — Indictments over $20 have right to trial by jury

T — Too much bail, excessive fines, cruel punishment prohibited

E — Enumeration of certain rights does not deny others
S — States or the people reserve all other rights

Abraham Lincoln's first vice-president—Abra**ham Lin**coln—
Hannibal Hamlin

The 11 Confederate states, in order of secession—
Several **M**en **F**ought **A**gainst **G**eneral
Lee **T**o **V**aunt **A**rrogant **N**orthern **T**raits.
Jon A. Bethel, Houston, Texas

S — South Carolina
M — Mississippi
F — Florida
A — Alabama
G — Georgia
L — Louisiana
T — Tennessee
V — Virginia
A — Arkansas
N — North Carolina
T — Texas

The heaviest president was Taft, who weighed well over 300 pounds. "Taft" rearranged spells "Fatt".

The Presidential Succession Act passed July 18, 1947 states that after the vice-president, the Speaker of the House, and the president pro tempore of the Senate, the sequence shall be the Cabinet members in order of the creation of their departments as follows—
See **T**he **D**og **J**ump **I**n **A** **C**ircle.
Leave **H**er **H**ome **T**o **E**ntertain **E**d.

S — State
T — Treasury
D — Defense (originally the War Department)
J — Justice (Attorney General)
I — Interior
A — Agriculture
C — Commerce
L — Labor

H — Health and Human Services
H — Housing and Urban Development
T — Transportation
E — Energy
E — Education

Campaign Slogans

Political slogans can be used as mnemonic devices to help member candidates, running mates, and issues.

The campaign of 1840—

Tippecanoe and Tyler Too.

This was used by the Whig party when William Henry Harrison, the hero of the Battle of Tippecanoe, was the Whig presidential candidate and John Tyler was his running mate.

The campaign of 1884—

A Public Office is a Public Trust.

This was used by the Democrats to remind the voters that James G. Blaine, the Republican candidate, was believed to have sold favors to a railroad while Speaker of the House in the 1870s.

The Republicans used "Ma, Ma, Where's my paw? Gone to the White House. Haw. Haw. Haw." to remind the voters that Grover Cleveland, Blaine's opponent and a bachelor, had admitted during the campaign to fathering an illegitimate child.

The Democrats countered with "Blaine. Blaine. James G. Blaine. The continental liar from the state of Maine."

The fact that Cleveland won probably demonstrates that the 19th century American voters preferred someone who fooled around in private and kept his public life clean, instead of the reverse. This seems to have changed, judging from recent presidential politicking trends.

The campaign of 1904—

Teddy Roosevelt used "A man, A plan, A canal, Panama," which is interesting because it set forth the issue of the potential construction of the Panama Canal, and also because it is a palindrome (spells the same thing backwards or forwards) created by Leigh Mercer.

The canal itself is backwards, in a way. The Atlantic end is further west than the Pacific end.

The campaign of 1936—

Alf Landon, running against Franklin Roosevelt (who was seeking his second term), used "Up with Alf—Down with the Alphabet," an aspersion cast at the proliferation of "alphabet agencies" set up in FDR's first term (e.g., WPA, SEC, TVA, etc.).

Electoral Vote

In a close election it is difficult to remember all the states that each candidate carried, but when it is lopsided it is easier to create a memory trick to remember who carried which states.

1936—

The states that Alf Landon carried in 1936 (a landslide for Franklin Delano Roosevelt)—

Massive **V**ote (against him)

M — Maine
V — Vermont

1964—

The states that Barry Goldwater carried in the 1964 election (a landslide for Lyndon Johnson) may be remembered by visualizing a door swinging shut and hitting Goldwater in the rear end—

GASLAM

G — Georgia
A — Alabama
S — South Carolina
L — Louisiana
A — Arizona
M — Mississippi

1972—

The electoral votes that George McGovern received in the 1972 election (a landslide for Richard Nixon) may be remembered by picturing a "mad" voter—

MaD

Ma — Massachusetts
D — District of Columbia

1984—

The electoral votes that Walter Mondale received in the 1984 election (a landslide for Ronald Reagan) may be remembered by creating an image of Mondale going fishing after the election—

HiM DiG WoRM

(disregarding the vowels)

H — Hawaii
M — Maryland
D — District of Columbia
G — Georgia
W — West Virginia
R — Rhode Island
M — Minnesota

Miscellaneous

During the Spanish-American War, the U.S.S. *Oregon* made the fastest trip then on record around Cape Horn to join the American fleet at the Battle of Santiago in 1898. The crew created an acrostic based on the ship's name—

Under
Steady
Steaming
Our

Run
East
Gained
Our
Name

Even though this was a record setting trip, it still took well over two months and was one of the reasons the United States undertook the construction of the Panama Canal.

The pioneering labor union that was organized in Chicago in 1905 was satirized in the press with the phrase—

I **W**on't **W**ork

The union's name was actually Industrial Workers of the World.

10

Mnemonic Devices
— for —
The Military

The various branches of the military use many acronyms and mnemonics to train recruits in the shortest amount of time. The use of acronyms has been a tradition of the Pentagon since before the Second World War. Just think of all the forms their use has saved (in triplicate).

Military Medals and Ribbons are a way of identifying what activities or campaigns a serviceman was engaged in. For example, the Congressional Space Medal of Honor, awarded to astronauts, may be identified by a 10 mm × 35 mm ribbon with symmetrical and vertical yellow, dark blue, light blue, and white stripes with a red stripe in the center. The British Defence Medal was awarded to those in Civil Defence in Great Britain who were subject to air attack from September 3, 1939 to May 8, 1945. The ribbon is flame colored with green edges with a narrow black stripe in each green edge. The reddish-orange symbolizes the fires caused by the bombing as well as the searchlights, the black is for the blackouts, and the British homeland is represented by the green.

You can remember the rank of Generals by visualizing Josephine caressing Napoleon and saying—

Be **M**y **L**ittle **G**eneral.

B — Brigadier — 1 star general
M — Major — 2 star general
L — Lieutenant — 3 star general
G — General — 4 star general

Military ranks of the Army (in ascending order)—

Privates **C**an't **S**alute **W**ithout **L**earning
Correct **M**ilitary **C**ommand **G**rades.
David Romanovsky, Vancouver, British Columbia

P — Private
C — Corporal
S — Sergeant
W — Warrant Officer
L — Lieutenant
C — Captain
M — Major
C — Colonel
G — General

There is a tradition used by sculptors of military leaders on horseback—

If the military leader was considered a man of action, then the horse will be shown rearing.

If the military leader was considered a man of authority, in other words more of an administrator, then all four of the horse's hooves will be on the ground.

The meaning of the letters above the left pocket of a soldier's uniform—

US ARMY

U — Uncle
S — Sam
A — Ain't
R — Released
M — Me
Y — Yet

The Marine island-hopping campaign in the Pacific in World War II can be remembered with the word—

BIGOT

B — Bougainville
I — Iwo Jima
G — Guadalcanal
O — Okinawa
T — Tarawa

The origin of the word "flak" is an acronym for the German artillery piece that was used in World War II—

FLiegerAbwehrKanone

which is translated as Flying Aircraft Cannon.

A word that started out as a military acronym but has entered our everyday language—

SNAFU

S — Situation
N — Normal
A — All
F — Fouled
U — Up

And finally, the primary types of National Defenses—

NBC

N — Nuclear
B — Biological
C — Chemical

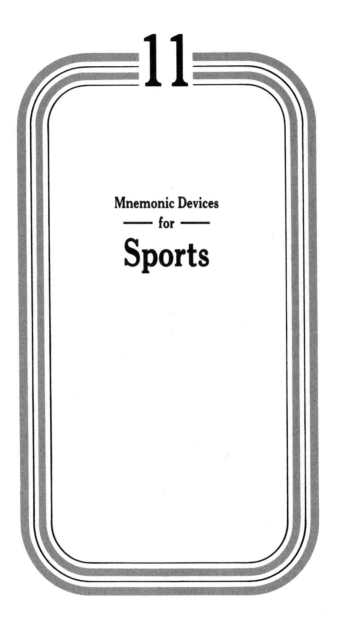

11

Mnemonic Devices
— for —
Sports

Sports trivia enthusiasts abound and most have their own methods of remembering obscure facts. What you will find here are a representative sample of how to remember facts about well-known athletes and events.

Mildred "Babe" Didrikson Zaharias (1914–1956) was almost without question the greatest female athlete of the 20th century. In the 1932 Olympic trials she won five events and set three world records. In the Olympics themselves, she won gold medals and set world records in the 80-meter hurdles and the javelin throw. She played on three AAU All-American basketball teams (for Dallas). She later took up golf and won 22 amateur events, including 14 in a row. She turned golf pro and won 34 tournaments, including three U.S. Opens. The way to remember her sports is—

Thank God for Babe

T — Track
G — Golf
B — Basketball

Baseball

The first inductees into Baseball's Hall of Fame in Cooperstown, New York, as selected by the Baseball Writers' Association of America in 1936—

Writers **C**ould **R**ate **M**en **J**ustly.

W — Wagner, Honus
C — Cobb, Ty
R — Ruth, Babe
M — Mathewson, Christy
J — Johnson, Walter

How to remember who stopped Joe DiMaggio's 56-game hitting streak (on July 17th, 1941)—

Ken **K**eltner **K**illed it in **C**leveland.

The year of baseball's last .400 hitter—

.41 in '41

Ted Williams hit .406 (rounded off is 41%) for the Boston Red Sox in the 1941 season.

The pitching strategy for the Boston Braves during the early 50s—

Spahn and Sain,
and pray for rain.

(Warren Spahn and Johnny Sain were their only two good pitchers; a corollary was formulated by the Kansas City Athletics in the '60s when their only good pitcher was Bud Daley—Pitch old Bud and pray for a flood.)

Where Casey Stengel came from—

Casey

Casey — K.C. — Kansas City (Born Charles Dillon Stengel in Kansas City, Mo., on July 30, 1891).

The year and the number of homers that Roger Maris hit when he broke Babe Ruth's single season record—

61 in '61

Also, Norm Cash led the major leagues in batting average that year with .361.

The last two thirty-game winners in major league baseball—
Dizzy and Denny

Jerome "Dizzy" Dean was 30-7 for the St. Louis Cardinals in '34 and Dennis "Denny" McLain was 31-6 for the Detroit Tigers in '68 (34 × 2). Each of their teams went on to win the World Series.

Basketball

Wilt Chamberlain's 100 point game (using 3's, 2's, and 6's) —

Played 3/2/62 in Hershey, Pennsylvania

Attempted 63 and made 36 field goals

Attempted 32 and made 28 free throws 25 rebounds, 2 assists

How to remember the four divisions of the National Basketball Association—

Alphabetical from the East coast to the West coast—

A — Atlantic
C — Central
M — Midwest
P — Pacific

Expansion teams will be entering the NBA in alphabetic order—

Charlotte   — 1988/89 season
Miami   — 1988/89 season
Minnesota — 1989/90 season
Orlando   — 1989/90 season

Bridge

One method of remembering the rank of suits in bridge bidding—
New Sweethearts Happily Dance Close.

N — No Trump
S — Spades
H — Hearts
D — Diamonds
C — Clubs

Fishing

How the wind affects fishing—

> When the wind is in the East,
> It's neither good for man nor beast.
> When the wind is in the North,
> The skillful fisher goes not forth.
> When the wind is in the South,
> It blows the bait in the fish's mouth.
> When the wind is in the West,
> Then it is at its very best.

How to catch a trout—

> The rod light and taper, thy tackle fine,
> Thy lead ten inches upon thy line;
> Bigger or less, according to the stream,
> Angle in the dark, when others dream:
> Or in a cloudy day with a lively worm,
> The Bradlin is best; but give him a turn
> Before thou do land a large wellgrown trout.
> And if with a fly thou wilt have a bout,
> Overload not with links, that the fly may fall
> First on the stream for that's all in all.
> The line shorter than the rod, with a natural fly:
> But the chief point of all is the cookery.

Thomas Barker (1651)

Football

Probably the most famous backfield in college football history was the Four Horsemen of Notre Dame fame (publicized by *New York Herald-Tribune* reporter Grantland Rice on October 19, 1924). You can recall their names by creating a mental image of—

A crow laid on the mill stool.

crow — Crowley
laid — Layden
mill — Miller
stool — Stuhldreher

Hockey

The four divisions of the National Hockey League—
PANS

P — Patrick (Wales Conference)
A — Adams (Wales Conference)
N — Norris(Campbell Conference)
S — Smythe(Campbell Conference)

Horse Racing

The eleven horses that have won Racing's Triple Crown (Kentucky Derby, Belmont, and Preakness in the same year) in order—

Surely Good Old War Widows Can Always
Cook Some Sour Apples.

S — Sir Barton (1919)
G — Gallant Fox (1930)
O — Omaha (1935)
W — War Admiral (1937)
W — Whirlaway (1941)
C — Count Fleet (1943)
A — Assault (1946)
C — Citation (1948)
S — Secretariat (1973)
S — Seattle Slew (1977)
A — Affirmed (1978)

The four jockeys with more than 6000 victories each—

Long Pink Shoe Cord

Long — Johnny Longden
Pink — Laffit Pincay
Shoe — Willie Shoemaker
Cord — Angel Cordero

What to do with horses with white markings—

> One white foot, run him for your life.
> Two white feet, keep him for your wife.
> Three white feet, keep him for your man.
> Four white feet, sell him if you can.
> Four white feet and a stripe on the nose,
> Knock him in the head and feed him to the crows.

There seems to be some validity to this. Horses with three or four white feet do seem to have a higher rate of injury.

The different types of horse gaits—

Who's **G**ot **T**rains? **C**anadian **P**acific **R**ailway.

W — Walk
G — Gallop
T — Trot
C — Canter
P — Pace
R — Run

Hunting

A rule for shooting—

> Never, never let your gun
> Pointed be at anyone.
> All the pheasants ever bred
> Won't make up for one man dead.

Steps in firing a rifle—

BRASSF

B — Breath
R — Relax
A — Aim
S — Stop breathing
S — Squeeze slowly
F — Fire

Poker

The sequence of winning hands (no wild cards)—the F hands all come together and the number of letters gives the order—

Straight **F**lush	—	13 letters
Four of a Kind	—	11 letters
Full House	—	9 letters
Flush	—	5 letters
Straight		
Three of a Kind	—	"three"
Two Pair	—	"two"
One Pair	—	"one"
High Card		

Note: Adding a wild card(s) creates one more "F" hand, Five of a kind, which is the highest hand of all.

Scuba

The word is an acronym for "**S**elf **C**ontained **U**nderwater **B**reathing **A**pparatus", but it can also can be remembered by—

Some **C**ome **U**p **B**arely **A**live

The way to remember how fast to come up from a deep dive — come up with the smallest bubbles (about one foot per second).

Snooker

How to remember how to set up the group of three colored balls in the back court of a snooker table (left to right) —

God **B**less **Y**ou.

G — Green ball (3 points) on the left
B — Brown ball (4 points) in the center
Y — Yellow ball (2 points) on the right

12

Mnemonic Devices
— for —
Business

Each type of business has a certain amount of slang and jargon that are meaningful only to insiders. Several areas which require certification, such as law, accounting, and brokering, use memory aids to assist in preparation for exams. Both the stock market and the data processing field have a large number of mnemonic devices which are discussed in this chapter in some detail.

The group of seven industrial nations, known as G7—

King Fran Can U JIG?

King — United Kingdom
Fran — France
Can — Canada
U — United States
J — Japan
I — Italy
G — Germany, West

OPEC (Organization of Petroleum Exporting Countries) member nations—

QUIK EVIL GAINS

Brian E. Schoot, Brookfield, Ill.

Q — Qatar
U — United Arab Emirates
I — Indonesia
K — Kuwait

E — Ecuador
V — Venezuela
I — Iran
L — Libya

G — Gabon
A — Algeria
I — Iraq
N — Nigeria
S — Saudi Arabia

Auditors are trained to uphold certain auditing standards when preparing certified financial statements. These can be remembered by the silly phrase—

TIPSIE WACI

T — Training
I — Independence

P — Professional care
S — Supervision and planning
I — Informative disclosure
E — Evidence
W — Whole, Financial statements taken as a
A — Adherence to GAAP (Generally Accepted Accounting Practices)
C — Consistency
I — Issue an opinion

Advertising/Marketing

On the value of advertising—

> The codfish lays a million eggs,
> The helpful hen lays one.
> The codfish makes no fuss at all,
> The hen boasts what she's done.
> We forget the gentle codfish,
> The hen we eulogise;
> Which teaches us this lesson that—
> It pays to advertise!

The four steps in marketing a product—
AIDA

A — Attention — get the attention of the consumer
I — Interest — develop his interest
D — Desire — create a desire for the product
A — Action — stimulate a course of action by the consumer

An Advertising Agency song—

> When your client's hopping mad
> Put his picture in the ad.
> If he still should prove refractory
> Add a picture of his factory.

Data Processing

Mnemonic has a special meaning as a data processing term. It stands for the code assigned to a particular command that the programmer instructs the computer to perform. For example, the mnemonic for the Branch on Index Low or Equal assembly language command is **BXLE**. It is easier to remember than the machine language operation code **87**, since there are dozens of different instructions, each having a mnemonic op code indicating what type of computer command is to be performed.

In the data processing field, a way to remember the divisions of a COBOL program—

In **E**very **D**amn **P**rogram

or

I Eat **D**ill **P**ickles.

I — Identification division
E — Environment division
D — Data division
P — Procedure division

A bit is an acronym for a binary digit; the method to remember the number of bits in a byte (one addressable storage location)—

8 bits to the byte

The term "nibble" is also used to represent 4 bits, in which case there are 2 nibbles to the byte.

The term that relates the quality of the data input to the quality of the data output (which also applies to any other field of endeavor)—

GIGO

G — Garbage
I   — In,
G — Garbage
O — Out

The recommended method for designing data processing systems and writing programs—

KISS

K — Keep
I   — It
S — Simple,
S — Stupid

(The rock group KISS was named for Kings In Satanic Service)

Thomas Watson, Sr. (the man that put IBM on the map) had a brainstorm at an IBM Hundred Percent Club banquet that was later printed and given to all IBM salesmen—

The Five C's
. . . "that we must possess if we want to do our full share."

Conception
Consistency
Cooperation
Courage
Confidence

John Patterson, founder of the National Cash Register Company (NCR), taught his salesmen to present the five benefits of a data processing system by using the word—

SPICE

S — Service
P — Profits
I — Information
C — Convenient
E — Economical

What IBM meant in the transfer-happy days of the 1960s and '70s—

I've Been Moved

IBM's strategy to sell DASD (Direct Access Storage Devices) has been said to be to create a desire in their customers for **Lalalod**—

Lots and Lots and Lots of Data

Legal

The common-law felonies—

MR. & MRS. LAMB
William A. Freedman, San Gabriel, Calif.

M — Murder
R — Rape
M — Manslaughter
R — Robbery
S — Sodomy

L — Larceny
A — Arson
M — Mayhem
B — Burglary

Twelve legal ways to gain or lose title—
A Busy Court G. McSoft, J.P.

A — Administration
B — Bankruptcy
C — Contract
G — Gift or Grant
M — Marriage
C — Custom
S — Succession
O — Occupancy
F — Forfeiture
T — Testament
J — Judgment
P — Precognitive

Policemen are taught the exceptions to when a search warrant is needed with the phrase—
COP IS ME

C — Consent
O — Open view
P — Public place

I — Incidental to a lawful arrest
S — Stop and frisk (a suspicious person)

M — Mobil premises
E — Emergency

The doctrine of "adverse possession" by which one party can acquire a part of his neighbor's property (if the property is adjoining) and if the conditions have been met for ten years may be remembered by—
COHEN

C — Continuous usage
O — Open usage
H — Hostile usage (not shared in common)
E — Exclusive usage
N — Notorious usage

Restaurant

Old English inns kept a box near the door to remind customers that, if the service was good, a little extra money for the waiter might be appropriate. The boxes were labeled "To Insure Promptness" but the phrase was quickly reduced to the initials—

T.I.P.

On the value of cooking meat containing fat—

No waste, no taste

Here are some cooking hints that may come in handy in the kitchen—

Oysters "**R**" in season during months containing "**R**."

A pint of water weighs a pound and a quarter (an imperial pint as used in Canada and the United Kingdom, that is).

A pint's a pound, the world around. (16 fluid ounces)

Cooking rice? Water's twice. (2 cups of water for one cup of rice)

One big T equals teaspoons three.

After melon, wine is felon.

Wine upon beer, I counsel thee
Beer upon wine, let that be.

Beer on whiskey, mighty risky.
Whiskey on beer, never fear.

How to pass food dishes at the dinner table—left to right is right.

Stock Market

This is a sound strategy for making money in the Stock Market. Sounds easy, doesn't it?

Be BuLliSH.

B — Buy
L — Low,
S — Sell
H — High

And don't forget these stock market directions—

You have to **Bear Down**, when the **Bull** kicks **Up**.

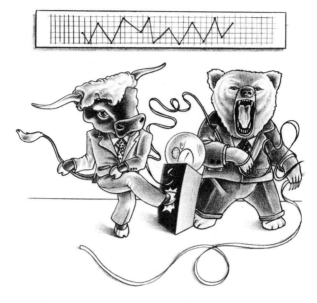

Here are some other stock market animals (Zero Coupon Bonds) that can be found roaming the halls of various brokerage houses—

CATS

C — Certificate
A — Accrual
T — Treasury
S — Security

from Salomon Brothers

TIGR

T — Treasury
I — Investment
G — Growth
R — Receipts

from Merrill Lynch

LION

L — Lehman
I — Investment
O — Opportunity
N — Note

from Lehman Brothers

The Securities Act of 1934 was passed by Congress reacting to the excesses of brokers and investors in the 1920s. The provisions of the act may be remembered with this phrase—

SIMMRS PAN

S — SEC established
I   — Insiders requirements
M — Manipulations prohibited
M — Margin requirements
R — Registration of bid
S — Short sale rule

P — Proxy statement   < Required of all
A — Annual report   < registered
N — Net Capital rule   < companies

Ranking of Treasury Instruments (in descending order by length of maturity)—

Bad News, Charlie Brown

B	— Bonds	—	10–30 years
N	— Notes	—	1–10 years
C	— Certificate	—	1 year
B	— Bill	—	3-6-12 months

The allocation of orders for Municipal Bond sales (according to Rule G-11 of the MSRB)—

Peggy Got Goosed DownTown.

P — Presale orders
G — Group—Net orders
G — Group—Less concession orders
D — Designated orders
T — Take-down orders

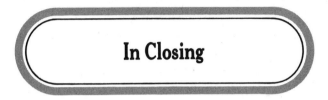

In Closing

Finally, a few words of sound advice (excuse the pun)—

> When in danger or in doubt,
> Run in circles, scream and shout.
>
> *Laurence J. Peter*

Acknowledgments

I wish to thank the many people over the years that have passed on to me some of their favorite mnemonic devices. I don't have a good way of remembering (the shame of it!) who mentioned each one first. I am grateful to Mike Rolon for his encouragement at a point when I was procrastinating about the future of this project. Jim Donovan has provided invaluable guidance both as editor and trivia buff. I especially want to thank those who have provided guidance with entire sections of this book. They are Dr. Dean Rising, Joyce Benne, and Rebecca Williams.

Others who were very helpful include my brothers, Clint, Mike, and Vince Benne; my children, Kimberly Benne Hawkins, Bart H. and Karen Benne; and (in approximate chronological order) George McCurdy, Jack Brustad, David Brooks, Dave and Karl Swierenga, Julie Denny Jenkins, Leora Sies, Deborah Molodofsky Williams, Randy Barner, Jay Welch, C.J. McManus, Jr., Ron Pierce, Amy McClintic, Jim Abrams, Dr. Charlie Watkins, Stephanie Young, Rev. Wes Lackey, Dave Phelps (King Arthur Jewelry), Bill Barniea, Jen Jahnke, Marta Montgomery, R.N., Brad Sham (KRLD), Rev. David Mack, Kevin Sullivan, Ted Fishman, John Altmann, Sheldon Lord, Barbara and Sam Hegler, Dick Curran (AA), Tom Perkowsky (AA), David Shapp, Gerrit Quambusch (Loews Anatole), Hubert Aaron (Park Central Bank), Chuck Fenster, Werner Perret (Germany), Simon and Victoria Tilbury (England), Alex Burton (KRLD), Curt Hildebrand (AAA), Susan Courbier (France), Frances Casey, Isaac Asimov, Ted Buck, Bob and Diane Ganson, Frank Roys, Mike Miler, Ralph Steckel, Bob Vaughn, Taylor Barton, Paula Lawson, Dr. James Rising, Bryce D. Segar, Sara Jo Mueller, Bob Weidman, Bill Pawson, Max E. Benne, Carolyn Nesbitt (Shelton School), Carol and Joe Utay, Nancy Redington, Nancy Kruh (Dallas Morning News), Michelle and Csaba Lepp, Chuck Hemry, Beth Stewart (Plano Sr. High), R.W. Beene, Glenn Fischer, Suzanne Mihelich, Sami Mikhail, Mark Glomstead, Bill Farmer, Russ Hicks, Bill Sklar, Ken Terrell (Delta), Madeleine

Marr (New York), Tim Ricks (AA), Erin Donnelly (AA), John Cosgrove (AA), Suzie Gurley (Wordware), Ryan Houlgate (TI), Cyndie Rohde (TI), Joyce Leraas, Alicia Bramley, Deanna and Dana Lepp, Lou Mayfield, Betty Starnes, Lara Stripling, Kara Williams, John Lapp, Jane Cohen, Susan Barlowe, Scott McClintic, Susan Rappaport, Craig Gardner, Joel Wall, Alex Whitman, Sgt. Doug Kowalski (DPD), Jerry Lucas, Stephen Wolf, Hugh Ferguson, Mary Keen, Dale Hansen, Jim Livingston, Les Hodson, Jeff Seib, and Robert West, Jr.

Those who have communicated mnemonic devices to me by mail include Paul Smith (Dallas), Wade Gates (Weatherford), Katherine L. Robinson (Grapevine), Ralph Cruz (Dallas), Kit Odum (Lewisville), Nancy Rempe (Dallas), Tricia Kraemer (Plano), Susan Schofer Johnson (Grapevine), Dwight L. Bates, D.P.M. (Dallas), G.W. Bruffey, Jr. (Plano), Cindy Henderson (Plano), Richard K. Ryalls (Carrollton), Lloyd S. Gastwirth (Dallas), Fredna B. Baird (Dallas), Roy L. Moskop (Dallas), Donald S. Stark (Duncanville), Chris Holmberg (Dallas), Arnold Romberg (Dallas), Ann Cunningham (Dallas), Jennette Womack (Dallas), Chris Ciaglia (Plano), Teresa Horne (Grapevine), Arlie M. Skov (Anchorage, Alaska), Robert J. Kalina (Euless), Rick Krause (Dallas), Nancy Lee Timmins (Dallas), Theresa Overall (Richardson), Jerry Anderson (Duncanville), William H. Julian (Leesburg), Daniel Polk (Dallas), Dr. Graydon H. Doolittle (Norman, Oklahoma), Larry Knight (Carrollton), Maxine Plummer (San Angelo), and Randall Beggs (Dallas).

I would also like to thank, in advance, those people who will send other interesting memory aids to me at the following address:

Bart Benne
Attention: WASPLEG II
P.O. Box 832401
Richardson, Texas 75083

Bibliography

American Heritage Dictionaries, Editors, *Word Mysteries & Histories,* Houghton Mifflin Co., Boston, Mass., 1986

Associated Press Sports Staff, Editors, *The Sports Immortals,* A Rutledge Book, div. of Prentice-Hall, Englewood Cliffs, N.J., 1972

Brett, Simon, Editor, *The Faber Book of Useful Verse,* Faber & Faber, London, 1981

Cermak, Laird S., *Improving Your Memory,* W.W. Norton & Co., New York, N.Y., 1975

Crypton, Dr., *Timid Virgins Make Dull Company,* Viking Penguin Inc., New York, N.Y., 1984

Cutler, Daniel S., *Ten Zebras Bit My Cheek,* Hot Dogs! Ink, Ann Arbor, Michigan, 1981

Dorling, H. Taprell, *Ribbons and Medals,* Doubleday & Co., Garden City, N.Y., 1974

Eyre Methuen editors, *Dictionary of Mnemonics,* Eyre Methuen, London, 1972

Higbee, Kenneth L., *Your Memory—How it works and how to improve it,* Prentice-Hall Inc., Englewood Cliffs, New Jersey, 1977

Lane, Hana Umlaud, Editor, *The World Almanac and Book of Facts,* Newspaper Enterprise Association, New York, N.Y., 1986

Lorayne, Harry and Lucas, Jerry, *The Memory Book,* Ballantine Books, New York, N.Y., 1974

Military Service Publishing Co., *The Officer's Guide—10th Edition,* Harrisburg, Pennsylvania, 1944

Omni Magazine Games column, Scot Morris, editor

Rogers, William, *THINK-A Biography of the Watsons and IBM,* Stein and Day, New York, N.Y., 1969

Safire, William, *On Language,* Avon Books, New York, N.Y., 1980

Sanderson, Inc., *Private Pilot Manual,* Jeppesen Sanderson, Inc., Denver, Colorado, 1977

Simons, Janet A., Irwin, Donald B., Drinnin, Beverly A., *Psychology-The Search for Understanding,* West Publishing Co., St. Paul, Minnesota, 1987

Smith, Bernie, *The Joy of Trivia,* Brooke House, Los Angeles, California, 1976

Smith, Huston, *The Religions of Man,* Harper & Row, New York, N.Y., 1958

Suid, Murray, *Demonic Mnemonics,* Pitman Learning, Inc., Belmont, Calif., 1981

Young, Morris and Gibson, Walter, *How to Develop An Exceptional Memory,* Wilshire Book Company, North Hollywood, Calif., 1962

Index